The Practice
of
Home

The Practice
of
Home

Biography of a House

Charles Goodrich

 The Lyons Press
Guilford, Connecticut
An imprint of The Globe Pequot Press

Acknowledgments:
Some of these essays have been previously published, sometimes in different forms:
"Night Canoe" in *Northern Lights:* Vol. IX, Number 4, Winter, 1994.
"Fathering the Night" in *The Sun,* Issue 230, February, 1995.
"Home Birth" in *The Sun,* Issue 246, June, 1996.
"Remodeling the Hovel" in *The Sun,* Issue 320, August, 2002.
"To Build a House" in *Open Spaces Quarterly,* Vol. 5, Issue 1, 2002.
"Grass Man" in *Best Essays Northwest,* Guy Maynard and Kathleen Holt, editors, University of Oregon Press, Eugene, 2003.

The Lyons Press is an imprint of The Globe Pequot Press.

Printed in the United States of America

10 9 8 7 6 5 4 3 2 1

The Library of Congress Cataloging-in-Publication Data is available on file.

ISBN 1–59228–416–7

For Kapa and Elliot,
and to the memory of Sarvahara Judd

Our soul is an abode, and by remembering *houses* and *rooms,* we learn to *abide* within ourselves.

—Gaston Bachelard

Indeed, as soon as the least of us stands still, that is the moment something extraordinary is seen to be going on in the world.

—Eudora Welty

By Way of Thanks

Gratitude to the loyal comrades of my writing groups, Rich Borsten, Gregg Kleiner, Kathleen Dean Moore, Steve Radosevich, Anita Sullivan, and Gail Wells, fine writers all. Poet and carpenter Clemens Starck has tried for two decades to help me make my writing straightforward and clear. May he keep trying. Thanks also to Chris Anderson, Tracy Daugherty, Marjorie Sandor, and Keith Scribner, talented writers and dedicated teachers at Oregon State University. Thanks to editors Penny Harrison, Guy Maynard, Sy Safransky, and Andrew Snee who gave me early feedback and support for my writing, and to Lilly Golden, whose deft suggestions, persistent friendship, and good cheer helped sustain me through a complete rewriting of the manuscript.

Thanks to Fishtrap, Literary Arts, Inc., and the Oregon Arts Commission for fellowships that helped support the writing of this book.

To my neighbors, I owe special thanks for showing me so many genuine ways to practice home. Community requires both openness and a certain degree of enclosure, and the tug between complete candor and a careful reserve is ever present in my mind as I write about real people. I'm not going to name my friends and neighbors individually here, and I have changed most of their names in this book. Though some of them would be pleased to be acknowledged by name, others would prefer to maintain their privacy, so I'm going to err on the side of discretion and simply thank them as a group. Friends, believe me, you are the better practitioners of home.

My community of practice begins anew every morning with my wife, Kapa Korobeinikov, and my son, Elliot. They are the warmth of my hearth.

Contents

Prologue: *The Practice of Home*

Some years ago I set out to build a small house. My plan was to do most of the labor myself, partly because I didn't have much money, but more important, because I wanted to try my hand at every aspect of home building. I wanted to be my own architect, stay up late sketching floor plans and elevations, studying how to maximize solar gain, optimize window placement, and minimize costs. I wanted to be my own general contractor, figure out how much lumber to buy and where to buy it, what kind of roofing materials to use, and which door hinges work best and why. I wanted to get inside the carpenter's art, to learn how to mark up the layout boards for framing the walls, and to try cutting the bird's mouth into the tails of the rafters where they'll sit on the wall plate. I wanted to wire my own switches and outlets so I'd have a feel for the flow of electricity within my walls. I wanted to sweat my own copper pipes and plumb my own toilet. I wanted to see if anything in me rose to the challenge of finish work, to know if I had cabinetmaking in my own makeup. I wanted to discover whether building a house could be a way of building a self.

During those years I worked half-time as the gardener for the county courthouse in the center of town, a job that left me time and energy to work on my house. The modest wages I earned every month went mostly into tools or two-by-sixes, cedar siding or fiberglass insulation, finish nails, linoleum, or paint. I worked by myself for two and a half years to build my seven-hundred-square-foot bachelor's bungalow, and then I met the woman whose husband I would become. Kapa shared my penchant for learning new skills, for searching out the satisfaction hidden in every kind of labor. She was as passionate as I was about gardening, she loved camping and hiking, and she was no slouch with a hammer either. During our first falling-in-love summer together, we backpacked all over the high Cascades, canoed insignificant rivers, climbed by moonlight to the lip of Mount St. Helens' smoking crater.

But come Labor Day, we buckled on our tool belts and began working twelve-hour days side by side to get a sleeping loft built and the solarium framed up before the autumn rains began. And so my house became *our* house, and since then Kapa and I have added a two-story addition, a big front porch, arbors and fences, and ever more gardens. Still, it didn't occur to me to write about building the house until our son, Elliot, was born here. His birth seemed to animate the house in ways I couldn't imagine when I first drew up my blueprints.

Before I first began building, I had envisioned a little bungalow that would be like the hard shell of a seed within which I could be the quiet germ of possibility, writing poems and minding my own business. And since I could not imagine ever making much money from my writing, I hoped the house would insulate me somewhat from our predatory economy. At that time I did not suspect that a house could be so much more than a shelter from the elements and proof against debts, couldn't imagine that my house would lead me out on unforeseen adventures.

In the process of building my house, I learned that I like doing carpentry and wiring and plumbing, but what I really love is *homing,* the daily practice of all the interwoven arts and skills of home. Home, it turns out, is a totally experimental process, sometimes scientific and sometimes slapstick. Home is where I can try anything; it's the first and best place to make mistakes. But I've also come to regard the practice of home as a kind of healing art, a practice whose goal is to strengthen the body of the community. Moreover, the ordinary chores and the odd adventures of home can serve as the occasions of a spiritual practice, too. In the words of the great Japanese teacher Dogen Zenji, "When you find your place where you are, practice occurs." Wherever home happens, practice happens. In fact, the practice of home may be nothing more than becoming a student of what holds things together.

So I want to recommend the practice of home as a kind of adventure, as travel of the most demanding and rewarding sort, for the practice of home leads us deeper and deeper into our own communities, into our native intelligence, and into our souls.

I built a house. I botched a lot of things, but all in all it came out all right. Let me tell you about it.

C. G.

Corvallis, Oregon

Home Birth

I'm sitting at the kitchen table, staring at the wood floor. Some of the gaps between the planks are so wide I could wedge the spine of a *National Geographic* into them. I went to great lengths to cinch those boards tight when I laid them, but the two-by-six tongue-and-groove hemlock has shrunk. If I got down on my knees and peered into one of those cracks, I would be looking into a working ecosystem: hair, dust, oats, rice, poppy seeds, insects dead and alive. I'm usually oblivious to moderate amounts of house dirt, but right now I'd like to squeegee thick varnish into these cracks, decoupage the whole damned floor.

I am haunted by this house. Kapa and I built it, are still building it, and now I'm infested with fantasies of additions and harried by fix-it lists. There are so many things I would have done differently and so many possibilities never explored. One morning over coffee I'll imagine building a window-filled breakfast nook out from the north wall of the kitchen. Another day our bedroom window will blossom into French doors and a walled courtyard will beckon to me. Could it be, I sometimes wonder, that I have been dreamed into being by the spirit of the house in order to fashion it a body of gypsum and wood?

The fact is, I don't want a walled courtyard off my bedroom. I have no desire for a larger kitchen. But remodeling ideas—practical or fantastic, humble or palatial—inhabit my psyche like fungus in cheese. I'm shot through with house.

Knot House, we call it, as if to make a virtue of our using low-grade, knot-riddled pine, hemlock, cedar, oak, and fir. Since the blemished appearance of our bargain lumber is so conspicuous, we've tried to elevate it to a style. Knotty lumber is all I could afford when I started building the house, but I would have chosen it anyway. Each knot is the root of a branch, where the tree has turned its energy outward from trunk to limb, a tricky maneuver. I've always been fascinated by the way the grain swirls around knotholes, just as I love the crows' tracks around Kapa's eyes, or the little scar on Elliot's knee where he burned himself with a campfire twig. I like the imperfect, the blemished, the compromised, in lumber as much as in people. Gazing into the knots in the pine flooring is like gazing into a map. It's a way to experience the longing for a home without leaving it. The cedar ceiling upstairs is fantastically spangled with knots and grain-whorls like sprawling nebulae in a honey-colored sky, a sort of slow, organic Van

Gogh. I've worked through many knots in my relationships, my writing, my ambitions, and my responsibilities to the world lying on the daybed gazing into the constellations of that ceiling.

We call it Knot House also to conjure the image of a knotted rope, the house as a kind of willing bondage that holds us tight to the spinning earth, holds together our private and our social lives, our secret desires and our public faces. And, after Elliot was born here at home, Knot House for the knotted umbilical cord, that rope of flesh I cut and the midwife tied.

It's the evening of Elliot's birth, and Kapa has been in labor all day. Her contractions have slowed and now she dozes between them. The living room's foldout couch has been opened into a double bed, and her four best friends sit in a half circle at the foot of the bed, talking among themselves, one knitting, another rubbing Kapa's feet. Although they are my friends, too, tonight they are devoted to being my wife's attendants, here as counselors and comforters, witnesses and nurses, cooks and cleaning ladies. Each woman seems completely relaxed and at home, as if attending at births were her true purpose. But I feel somewhat out of the loop. Maybe I'm disoriented by sleeplessness. Maybe anticipation and worry have tuned me to a totally different key. But whenever I pass one of the women on the way to make tea or fetch a blanket, she seems so solid and present, whereas I feel like a ghost watching it all happen, unnoticed by anybody else.

Siri, the midwife, sits at the kitchen table recording her notes. She is a slight, wiry woman, her frizzy blond hair tied back with a green and gold silk scarf. Her face has a lot of weather in it, and her manner is Quaker. She is worried a little about this slowdown, but she knows Kapa needs rest so she does not urge her to be on her feet just now.

My role at this birth has become so attenuated. Most of the day I have just shadowed Kapa, holding her when she wished to be held, steadying her while she swayed and crooned through contractions, staying away when the touchy transition stage left her feeling ferociously alone. Among these six women and their female aromas, in the dim light of the candles and the steamy heat of the woodstove, I feel dumb, diffuse, and entirely expendable.

I take out a pencil and begin to sketch an addition. A simple, rectangular room, twelve feet by sixteen. A study where I can shelve all my books, where I can close the door and do my writing. Here's where my desk would go, and here's a good place for a daybed. I figure out how to join the shed roof onto the south wall of the addition, just below the upstairs windows. The new room will get plenty of sun—I place several windows on the south and east walls and imagine myself working there at dawn, drinking my coffee while Kapa and the baby sleep late. I go into the hallway and see that, yes, I can punch a doorway into the study right here. I start making a list of the lumber I'd need. I make a note to buy a new chop saw.

I'm lying inside a big cardboard box, Elliot's house, made from the carton our new chest freezer was delivered in. I've been holed up for half an hour or so, reading and daydreaming, while just outside one-and-a-half-year-old Elliot pours his dozen Matchbox cars between two sauce pans and stirs them with a wooden spoon. Every few weeks we move the box to a different room to restore its novelty. Right now it is crowded into a corner of the living room where its flat roof serves as a folding table for clean laundry. There's enough light to read by in here, from the three window openings I cut into the cardboard. I lie back, browsing a book on vernacular architecture from around the world, looking at photos of simple stone houses in the Himalayas, their plastered walls the color of cardboard, their flat roofs piled high with dried yak dung.

I can't stretch my legs out straight, but there is a pillow, and for the time being I'm comfortable. None of us slept well last night. This is the first time all morning that Elliot has settled into solitary play. I know that if I crawl out and try to wash the breakfast dishes he will immediately come weasel in between the kitchen counter and my knees and beg, "Up, Papa. Up!"

So I remain captive in his house, angry at him for being so clingy, for screaming all night when his new tooth pushed at his gums, and also proud at how perkily he stirs his car soup. Imprisoned or not, I'm grateful for the rest. Later I'll bundle him out to the shop and try to interest him in playing with lumber scraps while I repair the leaky-roofed bird feeder. For now I'm content to lie here in this house within a house, looking at pictures of wickiups and igloos, soddies and cliff houses, huts, yurts, and cave dwellings.

Working alone late one afternoon during my first September of building the house—this is several years before I met Kapa—I'm hurrying to finish the roof sheathing, worn out from my unslacking labor and anxious about an impending autumn storm, when I step between two rafters and tumble sideways. As I fall across the exposed two-by-tens, I hear wooden, snapping sounds—three of my ribs cracking. I pull myself back onto the plywood and sit hunched over, my breathing constrained by sharp spikes of pain. Finally I see my neighbor Barb come around the house to move her lawn sprinkler. "Barbara!" I bleat, "I'm hurt." She fetches her husband, Ned, and they ease me down the ladder, into their car, and up to the hospital.

It feels odd, the next day, to be sitting in a lawn chair, watching, as five of my friends finish sheathing the roof. The storm is still gathering over the Coast Range, and batches of crows keep blowing up from the south, cawing ominously overhead. I have been told that I have a very goofy grin on my face from the Darvon. My eyeballs feel wet and chilly. I blame my moist eyes on the painkiller, but, in truth, it is from the kindness of my friends, who have set aside their busy schedules and assembled here on short notice to finish my roof before the rain arrives. My gratitude, as I watch the house progress while I do nothing, is complicated with a stunning sense of stupidity and undeserving.

One year later, in the process of installing my toilet, I pinch a nerve in my lower back. I lay motionless on the bathroom floor for three hours, every slight movement sending a jolt of pain throughout my body, until at last my muscles unclench just enough so that I can crawl to the front door. "Barbara! Barbara!" I cry, until she hears me. She backs her car across the lawn, right up to my doorstep, and looks down at me, bent over at 90 degrees and unable to straighten up one inch.

"Where to?" she asks me, then eases me into the backseat and drives me to her chiropractor. That good doctor asks several scheduled patients to wait while he tips me onto his table and leaps against my clenched spine, to no avail. When he tips me back to the floor, I am still locked into a right angle. Having failed to unfold me, thinking now of his patients in the waiting room, he lays a kindly hand on my shoulder, and says, "Would you mind leaving by the back door?"

And the following autumn, the year before I met Kapa, when I had moved into the unfinished house but was still hanging interior doors and building kitchen cabinets, I lost September to the flu, then pneumonia.

Now Kapa, Elliot, and I always go camping in the autumn. We leave summer's long list of unfinished chores to mutter to itself on the refrigerator, while we go play in the mountains for a couple of weeks. Upon returning, when I first walk in through the back door and smell the unstirred air, and hear how deeply quiet the rooms have been in our absence, I sense that the house has made good use of its solitude. The wiring and plumbing feel rested, even the paint and varnish seem refreshed.

The door stands open behind me. Kapa is coming in noisily with the first load of gear. I feel the house sigh, take a long, deep breath, and welcome us home.

It's 4 a.m. A winter storm is flapping its wet fur against the windows. The candle shivers. *dusk – turning on the lights*
This is my favorite hour to be with the house—not just in it, but *with* it, partaking together in the exhilaration of the wind and rain. Out there, the house suffers the slap and chill of the storm's flung buckets. Its clapboards swell and close ranks shoulder to shoulder. The roof's three-tab shingles dig into each other with tarred fingers and hold on.

All the while, the inward face of the house remains unperturbed. Each tentative idea this room entertains is a tremulous candlelight shadow on the ceiling. The carpet lies deep in thought, obsessed with small details. The walls stand quietly, practicing their old martial art, swaying on the balls of their feet ever so slightly when the wind gusts.

Why not consider a house animate? Why not relate to it as a living being? Why not honor a house with a name and treat it with common decency and good manners? These days the vacuum cleaner looms particularly large in Elliot's mind. At any moment of the day he will point to its cubbyhole under the stairway and pronounce its name, "Wakuum Keena." This noisy beast who comes out once a week to graze on the rugs and prod its long snout under the sofa has far more reality for Elliot than his teddy bears. I believe he may regard the kitchen table as a living being; may think of his high chair, our double bed, the bathtub, certainly the toilet, as strange and powerful cousins who don't necessarily speak our language or eat when we eat, but who nevertheless have some peculiar status in the household. Should I cultivate that sensibility? Should I address Wakuum Keena by name and drag it about with some gentleness? Should I open the cabinet that houses the stereo and television with some ceremony, a flourish of the hand or a tiny bow?

I do bow at the back door whenever I come home. In fact, I've taken to making microscopic bows at any threshold, be it a friend's house, the grocery store, my bank. Some days I find myself paying obeisance in my mind to the bathroom sink for its equanimity, the refrigerator for its persistence, the bicycle for its swiftness and balance. It takes no energy. It isn't a political act, or a gesture of reverence. It just happens some days.

֎֎֎

Siri looks the baby over, suctions his throat, wipes the mucous from his mouth, and hands him to Kapa. With the baby on her belly, a change comes over her, as if her spirit has returned to the surface of her being after having dived down deep to help things along inside. A radiant heat pours from her.

Siri clamps two hemostats on the umbilical cord and asks if I want to cut it. We have discussed this in advance, and I have said I would like to, but when Siri holds the scissors out to me, I hesitate. It's brief, practically instantaneous, but it is one of those moments that open vertically, perpendicular to time, and encompass worlds. I have a fleeting vision of unknown ancestors and of generations of family yet to come—men, women, and children of every age and color, clothed in every imaginable way, every one of them looking at me rather sternly, watching me. All the different paths I might yet have taken had I not become a father will vanish at the moment when I sever that flesh, and so many connections, so many joys and burdens will be born.

I cut the cord with a steadiness of hand I do not possess. The experience leaves me calm and utterly clearheaded. A little bright blood—part mother, part son—shines on the blades.

When my time comes, I want to die in this house, with family and friends surrounding me as they surrounded Kapa during Elliot's birth. After my pulse is gone, let the mortician ferry me downtown and pump his infernal fluids into my veins. I won't quarrel if he uses a little rouge on my cheeks. Just dress me up in my fancy vest of cerulean blue silk that Kapa made for our wedding, and bring me back home.

I want to lie in the cheapest, knotty pine box (butt joints are fine) on sawhorses in the living room while my old friends lift a cup and tell lies about me. Let the able-bodied take a turn at the spade, then, and bury me out in the corner of the backyard, where the root weevils defeated our every attempt to garden, where we finally scattered wildflower seeds of which only daisies and poppies survive. Put a conservation easement on the property for my monument.

Kapa, I'd be thinking, the place is all yours now. I hope the gutters are holding up, the roof's intact, the doors still swing freely. Watch those front porch steps when they're wet! Remember to turn on the heat lamp in the pump house if the temperature drops below twenty. Tell Elliot he may have my old leather tool belt.

Fathering the Night

Carrying the baby horizontally across my chest like a football usually calms him, and often puts him to sleep. But not tonight. He's still crying, cycling through his whole repertoire: the screechy fear cry; the lower, throaty demand cry; some pitiful gasping interspersed with slobbery whimpers. Kapa nursed him an hour ago at midnight, so he isn't hungry. Teething, always suspect, doesn't seem to be the problem tonight; he isn't drooling much, nor is he clawing at his ears. I may give him a dropperful of Tylenol anyway, to help me relax.

I've already sung through my own repertoire of lullabies, gospel hymns, and ballads, and I'm getting hoarse. Singing, like acetaminophen, is an analgesic, but the anxiety I'm trying to ward off leaks out in blue lyrics about lost sailors, hanged thieves, worlds of woe. I recall Rosalie Sorrels's rendition of the classic antilullaby "The Baby Tree":

And when the stormy winds wail
And the breezes blow high in the gale
There's the funniest hoppin' and floppin' and droppin'
And fat little babes just hail

Sorrels, in the voice of the run-down mother reciting her griefs, tells us, "Every culture's got to have one—a hostile baby-rocking song."

Today is the day
We give babies away
With a half a pound of cheese . . .

My little loaf has fallen into a softer, hiccupy moaning now. How long we've been walking I can't say. Two hours? Probably less, but not much. I think he may drift off with another dozen turns around the carpet. I anticipate returning to bed, spooning up to Kapa's backside, absorbing her warmth.

Suddenly he's wailing again, and from the pit of my stomach comes a fleeting urge to hoist him over the railing and drop him down the stairwell.

His screaming escalates, the decibel level climbing, the pitch rising. This time I rise up with him, singing loud as church, harmonizing with his harsh cries. And to hell with him if he's scared. I'm scared, too.

Sometimes I feel
Like a motherless child
A long way from home
A long way from home

I remember my amazement in the first few weeks of his life when I discovered that he'd arrived with an entourage. The angels he watched in the corners of the ceiling were no surprise to me. I could see them—see something, anyway—as flitting smudges of light reflected at the edges of my glasses. It was the monsters and murderers he brought with him that I didn't anticipate. Images of disaster poured through my mind those first weeks. By day I was plagued with visions of Knot House burning, our car overturned. At night I dreamed of soldiers bayoneting babies, swinging babies by the heels into telephone poles. I had to quit listening to the radio news for a while. With the doors securely locked at night, I nevertheless heard footsteps in the kitchen more than once: my child's bad-ass cronies, his friends from the underworld, punks, shades.

And worst, day or night I would see myself slumped over the crib, my baby son face down and motionless there, not a drop of air in the room.

We're talking about a healthy, good-natured baby. A real sweetheart. A bright-eyed fudgsicle. A Buddha. No colic, no chronic ailments. Just good lungs and a fierce resistance to sleep. This child had his eyes open from the get-go. He watched the midwife pull the looped umbilical cord over his head so he could slither his lower half out. Placed in his mother's arms, he cased the joint before he nursed.

At the time, I presumed our most strenuous parental efforts would be aimed toward bringing him to consciousness, introducing him to the great waking world, but he needs no further propulsion in that direction from us. Instead we work at getting him to sleep, at holding him somewhat rooted in the netherworld he's just escaped. It is, of course, our need for sleep that drives us, just as his need for waking causes him to fight every drowse. Each evening he wrestles the sandman up to and over the brink of exhaustion, punching himself in the eyes all the way.

Nine months old now, he occasionally sleeps through half the night, waking just once for a midnight nursing. The anxiety that used to creep up on Kapa and me each evening toward his bedtime is mostly an uneasy memory. But, as when we look back on an extended visit by a difficult relative, we still fear that that unwelcome visitor may return.

Our neighbors burn a sulfurous security light over the clutter of their front yard, and its eerie glow is seeping in around the drawn drapes of our upstairs study, the room most distant from our bedroom, where Kapa is trying to sleep. The baby's also asleep, finally. After carrying him around the room, walking a mile or more while he screamed inconsolably, I resorted to hypnosis. I swayed back and forth so the yard light coming through the slit between curtain and wall fell across his face. Shadow to shadow I rocked, and the light played over his eyes like a copy machine. I xeroxed him to sleep.

There's a world map on the wall here. I tacked it up months ago so I could study it while I comfort him through his daytime crying jags. Sometimes I hold him tight and talk geography to him, naming all the major rivers of Africa, or saying over and over the names of the newly independent states of the Caucasus. One time, as I was crooning the names of the oceans to him, he suddenly quit crying, became very calm and, reaching out, placed a careful finger on the west coast of the island of Java.

Tonight I stand awhile before the map, waiting for his breathing to deepen, for the spasm of calm that always shakes his legs loose once he's sound asleep. I'm trying to trace the route of the hegira Kapa's parents made. Russian Old Believers, they were born in the Altai Mountains in Kazakhstan, but after their religion was outlawed by the Communists, they fled into northern China. That's where Kapa was born, near Kulja. Her father fought in the resistance, a chaotic civil war, until finally he had to flee the area, leaving his wife and children behind. With a hundred and fifty other Russians, he walked across the Gobi desert, over the Himalayas, through Tibet, and down into India, a four-year journey that only thirty-eight of the original refugees survived. I trace his route on this map often, recount his trials, and consider the enormous improbability of him making it to this country, of his family eventually being able to emigrate from northern China to Cleveland, Ohio, of Kapa ever becoming my wife. But tonight the yellow light from the window is too watery and dim. I can't make out any national boundaries, only the dark blotches of the continents and the paler expanses of the seas.

Other times as we tread the carpet, I recite to him our address. "Listen, little wiggler, we live in the catywompus house at 2340 Crystal Lake Drive, in the watershed of the Marys River, near the confluence of the Marys and the Willamette River, Corvallis—which comes from the Latin, *cor* meaning heart, and *vallis* meaning valley, so Corvallis means Heart of the Valley—State of Oregon, in the northwest corner of the USA, North America, Western Hemisphere, Earth, Solar System, Milky Way. This is your home. Remember that in case you ever get lost."

Or I try to rescue the crying hours by learning the constellations. It's winter, and the windows of our solarium look out upon the paths of Orion, Taurus, the Pleiades. When the baby cries, I take him to those windows and let him hurl his complaint at the stars while I tell him in a sleepy and, I dare hope, sleep-inducing monotone the snippets of Greek myths I've been reading at odd moments of the day. I point out Cassiopeia and tell him how she boasted of her beauty so outrageously that the sea nymphs complained to Neptune, who sent the sea beast Cetus (there he is, lower down, almost in the limbs of our cherry tree) to ravage the shores of Cassiopeia's country. Her husband, King Cepheus, consulted an oracle and learned that only by sacrificing their daughter, Andromeda, to the sea beast could he save his country. (There's Andromeda, in chains at her mother's feet.) Someday I'll tell him how Perseus rescued Andromeda, how he slayed Medusa, and how Pegasus, the winged horse, sprang from the Gorgon's snaky hair.

I tell him: Orion lusted after Atlas's beautiful daughters, the Pleiades, so Atlas bade Taurus come between them and keep the hunter at bay.

I tell him: Taurus is your sign, my little bullock. Now go to sleep.

Go to sleep.

🦎🦎🦎

4:30 a.m. The baby slept well, only crying out briefly two or three times. I feel rested. For once I rose at the alarm's first urging. I'm at my desk with several hours of solitude ahead before he and Kapa awaken. Outside in the dark garden a mild rain is falling with a sound like gentle static, a rough hand stroking long hair.

Coming into my small, crowded study from the relative spaciousness of the living room, I am aware of the abrupt change in atmosphere: the way the book-lined walls drink up sound, how the heavy air is permanently stained with the smells of my body, of dust and cheap incense, of the holy fragrance of ink on paper. My laboratory, my sanctum.

The baby, ten months old and crawling, is not ordinarily allowed in this room: it isn't baby-proofed. He is, of course, intensely curious about this off-limits space and will make a bee-line for the door whenever I leave it open. When I'm in here, I'll occasionally let him come in and conduct his own research, let him tug at the tangle of electrical cords under the computer, pluck at the strings of my guitar, pull dog-eared books from the bottom shelves, chew on my pens. He can never get enough of the wonders of his father's workroom, and he must always be carried out against his will, often crying.

In a year or two, this room will be his. It's the only room in the house suitable for his bedroom. I'll move my desk upstairs to share space with Kapa's drafting table and sewing machine, her watercolors and easel. Her room is in the addition we built together just before we married. It has a beautiful cedar ceiling, windows on all four walls, and plenty of room for my desk and files.

But as I write this, I realize that I don't want to give up my dark little study, my birthing chamber. I don't want to write in an open, airy, light-filled room. I want a close, dim space, crowded with books and saturated with the musk of labor. It takes time and effort to make a room smell like this.

He's standing at the crib rail, screaming. Twice already I've laid him down, rubbed his back, pulled the quilt over his shoulders. Both times he's bounced back up and resumed wailing as soon as I was horizontal. Kapa bailed out an hour ago, heading upstairs to try to get some sleep. I'm "on duty." I fluff the pillows around my head to muffle the din.

An infant's relentless crying seems so contrary to survival. I'm thinking not of nocturnal predators—leopards or hyenas drawn to the sound of small meat—but of the effects of sleep deprivation on parents. What law of nature drives the baby to unravel his caretakers' sanity? Like a pain that goes beyond its function of signaling damage, what's the purpose of this excess?

The how-to books are confident that letting baby "cry it out" will have the child sleeping through the night within a week. The principle is sound: don't reinforce baby's whims. The timeline, however, is a pediatric pipe dream. Three months since we started weaning him from his three-a-night nursings, he's now down to one, around midnight, and a semi-regular hour-long crying jag sometime between two and four. We've endured so many of these that we have learned to sleep through them—or, more precisely, to doze within them, as if inside a kind of sonic shell, a domed room with a ceiling made of jagged sound.

I dream that I'm trapped alone in a bombed-out building, all my comrades driven off or killed. I find a trapdoor, retreat down a shaft, and wriggle for hours through a stifling tunnel dark as a rifle bore. Finally the tunnel bulbs open into a small room. The darkness thins to dusty gray, then blooms deep scarlet and blue. A door opens. Three women in combat fatigues cross over to me and hold their hands out together, fingers lacing with mine in a cat's-cradle handshake.

"Congratulations," they all say, "you're going to have a baby."

He is nine days old. It's late morning, and I lie on the bed gazing at him, gloating. The skin of his eyelids is mottled a delicate lavender and rose. Little blotches of skin rash come and go from his cheeks. I believe if I watch carefully enough I might be able to see a patch emerge, bloom, and fade.

I can feel the tug of his attention. Even asleep he's sucking up sensations from the atmosphere, stretching his psyche, accruing experience. His milky irises may seem like barely congealed eternity, but they are here for specifics. Every day they become clearer and more faceted. He watches angels over my shoulder less often and instead studies my face.

When he cried before dawn I rose from bed and gathered him up. In my haste to comfort him, I left my glasses on the nightstand and, not wanting to waken weary Kapa, I walked him in a 20/200 blur: gauzy darkness, the furniture bulky and strange, the house itself anxious, tight shouldered, leaning in. I feared the creak of the floorboards would rouse him. I felt my way forward as if out onto the limb of a great tree.

❧❧❧

Dry lightning. Another spring storm is passing to the south. The baby, just three weeks old, sleeps in my lap, hot and heavy as a chunk of space debris, a cried-out little asteroid damp with perspiration. I stroke his furry head, marveling over the topography of his soft skull.

Sitting in the rocker before the broad solarium windows, I watch for the next flash of lightning, the next incarnation of the backyard. There—so windless and still it seems a tableau— the garden materializes, framed by small trees that Kapa chose and planted: *Magnolia stellata* by the grape arbor, *Styrax japonica* here beside the garden path, spirea and forsythia near the south fence, a grove of lilacs beyond the perennial border.

Under those lilacs is where we buried our first child, the thumb-sized fetus miscarried at three months. The baby in my lap would not have been conceived had that child lived. My mother lost her first child, a full-term baby strangled in delivery by the cord. After Elliot was born, we took the fresh placenta and blotted it on a canvas and saw a broad-headed oak tree. We buried the placenta under the little Japanese maple beside the mailbox.

I rock the baby and watch the sky. The lightning flashes last only a second, and then darkness returns with renewed depth. The garden reappears, ever so briefly, and bleeds back into the night.

To Build a House

The first house I helped build was a cabin on the Olympic Peninsula. The owners were old friends, squandering their college educations to move back to the land, raising chickens and kids, paying their bills by tree planting. Working on their house was the most forgiving of apprenticeships—their skills were as flimsy as mine. With a couple of how-to books, boundless energy, and inflated confidence, we were winging it. Something out of *The Hobbit* was what my friends had in mind, and cobbling was the method.

Cedar lumber we bought from a nearby homestead mill still had the bark on. It was so green that when we drove 16d sinkers into it, sap would squirt into our faces. They had no electricity up on that hilltop, so we cut studs and rafters to good-enough length with a chain saw. The cabin's front porch, with hexagonal windows like eyes on either side of the door, reminded me of a witch's face, and the whole house whistled when the wind blew.

The following year I was the hired hammer for another friend. This boat-tight little house was effectively a four-roomed cabinet, every never-to-be-seen-again nailhead countersunk and puttied, every hidden, underside surface sanded 120-grit smooth. My friend, a clinical psychologist detouring briefly into gardening and carpentry on his way to becoming a police detective, had a savage tongue. He'd cuss at the dumb lumber and hurl his hammer at the apple tree. But he was mild enough toward me and paid well, considering my ineptitude. It was he who taught me the sagest of carpenters' sayings: "Measure twice; cut once." Except he amended it in practice to "Measure twice, twice; cut once," and he passed on to me his clinical regard for clean, sharp tools.

A few years later I bought eleven acres of divvied-up farmland in a rural district southeast of Portland. The land had a small woodlot, a gentle knoll covered in good grass pasture, and, holy of holies, a tiny pond tucked in among old and very large cedar trees in the back of the property. I couldn't afford to bring power into the property, so, working entirely with hand tools, I cleared an opening in the trees where the land sloped down to the pond and began building a little cabin. I used twelve railroad ties half buried on end for foundation posts, and tied them together with four, rough-sawn six-by-eight beams. The cabin I built was only twelve feet by fifteen feet, but it felt roomy enough, with the ceiling vaulted up to the ridge of the saltbox roof. The north wall was just six feet high with one little window that peered down through the trees to a glimpse of the pond. I sat on a three-legged stool beside that window to eat my meals. The south-facing wall stood ten feet high and was chock-full of windows. A loft bed up near the ceiling left room for an open closet underneath. I had an old, round cast-iron woodstove named Toad, kerosene lanterns to read by, and a propane camp stove to cook on. My built-in desk faced out into the old hay field, where most mornings I'd see deer browsing.

That hermit phase lasted less than a year before I sold the land and the cabin and moved here to Corvallis. I wasn't thinking about building another house just then, but when my friend Andrew offered to sell me a lot he owned at the edge of town, I was tempted. I didn't think I had enough money to build a "real" house, a house that would meet the more expensive standards of the Uniform Building Code, but I drew up some plans and consulted another friend. Luke worked as a professional carpenter specializing in custom remodeling, a competitive business where a sharp pencil is just as critical as carpentry know-how. I showed him my detailed sketches of a straightforward twenty-four-foot-by-thirty-foot bungalow and asked him if my $14,000 cash would cover the cost of the materials. He chewed his pencil, scribbled some indecipherable numerals and said, "Yes. No question. You can do it."

So I started to build. First I put up a little pole building for a shop and storage shed. My friend Elmer was dismantling an old house in town, so I bought some hundred-year-old, straight-grained fir shiplap from him, and he helped me side my little shop building with it. I found a student in the architectural drafting program at the local community college to draw up my blueprints. I got an incredibly cheap bid on the concrete work, and once the foundation was finished, Andrew helped me frame the floor, install the rough plumbing, and lay the two-by-six car decking that would serve as my finished floor. I bought a secondhand front door, a thirdhand bedroom door, a used sink, used refrigerator, and stove. I built the bathroom cabinets of secondhand lumber and installed a beautiful, round, hand-thrown sink some potter friends had given me. I found an electrician to teach me the rudiments of wiring, then I installed all the circuits, fixtures, and outlets myself. I bought unframed, secondhand thermopane glass and built my own window sashes. Andrew and I put five coats of polyurethane on the hemlock floor and it came out looking glossy, yet old-fashioned, like a farmhouse floor.

Other friends put in hours and whole days of free labor. With their help I did all the carpentry myself. The two jobs I didn't feel competent to take on—the concrete work for the foundation and hanging all the sheetrock—I found others to do at bargain prices. I pinched every penny I could. Nevertheless, midway through construction, with the house dried-in—framed and sheathed, the roof on, doors and windows installed, but totally unfinished inside, the interior walls just skeletons of two-by-fours you could pass through—I was broke. I called up Luke. "Hey, Luke! You told me I had enough dough. What happened?"

"Oh," he said, "I knew your fourteen grand wouldn't go far."

"I'm not following you."

"You want to build a house, don't you? You'll find the money."

☙☙☙

The four-room bungalow I had in mind in those days was still closer to a hermitage than a tract house. I had a lot of help from my friends, but I also worked long hours alone, my love for solitude dovetailing with a reluctance to ask for too much assistance. Every evening I pored over my blueprints and reference books—books don't humiliate you for asking stupid questions—and laid out the next day's tasks. My minimal carpentry experience made me timid about directing the labor of others, so when friends did come to help, I was sometimes peeved by their presence, embarrassed to reveal my ignorance. I tended to hold their work to higher standards than I did my own. If somebody bent nailheads, I wouldn't say anything; I'd just go tear out his work and redo it after he'd gone.

Everyone commented on the small size of the house. "What if you get married and have kids?" they all wondered. But my immediate goal was a cheap, efficient bachelor's pad, a writer's refuge.

"If I meet the right woman," I'd always answer, "she can add on."

As soon as the front and back doors were hung and the toilet installed, I gave up my rented room in town to save money, and I moved into the half-finished house. I was working weekends as the supervisor for the local corrections work crew. Every Saturday and Sunday I'd take eight minor felons—men and women who had forged checks, been arrested too many times for drunk driving, or failed to pay child support—out to one of the county parks to rake leaves, spread gravel on pathways, or dig blackberry vines out of drainage ditches. Every payday

I'd buy some more materials and keep plugging along, installing fixtures, building kitchen cabinets, trimming out windows and doors.

Two years into the project, with the house comfortable if not entirely finished, I met Kapa. She liked my little bungalow, though there was hardly a corner that wasn't taken up with my stuff. The living room was set up as my study, dominated by bookshelves and a sprawling desk, and the kitchen counters were too high for her to work at comfortably. But we were in love, and rearranging the furniture could wait. We spent that first summer camping and backpacking every free moment, and by the time Labor Day came around, we'd decided to live together. Before my house would hold the two of us, however, we needed to frame up the solarium and add a sleeping loft above the living room. I bought Kapa a tool belt and we began working twelve-hour days, racing against the arrival of the autumn rains. A photograph I took of Kapa at the time shows her in overalls and tool belt, a pencil behind her ear, sawing a plank with the big Skil 77 circular saw, steady-eyed, set-lipped, and all business.

Kapa had built some furniture while in college and was handy with tools, scrupulous, even finical, in all her projects, while I was a slap-dash carpenter, competent at framing and rough stuff, but lacking the patience for finish work. In the early days of our relationship, we did not realize our potential for complementing each other's strengths and we often worked at cross-purposes. I would push Kapa to work faster than she wanted to and Kapa would pull at me to slow down and put more care into my work. Living in the little house together even as we worked on it gave us the opportunity to get to know each other at our worst. Even after I moved my many bookshelves and my huge writing desk from the living room to the bedroom (which became my study; we slept in the loft) and we set up Kapa's drafting table and easel in the solarium, Kapa still didn't feel like she had much personal space in the little bungalow. Our irritation with each other's different styles of working, exacerbated by the long hours we labored together, eventually undid us. Kapa moved out again, and we didn't speak for a year.

But eventually, cautiously, we renewed our relationship. Having weathered that long separation, we realized our connection was durable and deep, and within a few more months we'd decided to get married and start a family. But first we would need more space, so together we designed a two-story addition. The upstairs would be one spacious room with windows on all four walls. It would become Kapa's studio. Downstairs would be our new bedroom, and the little alcove in the hallway would be lined with built-in bookcases and we'd call it the library. As a bonus we planned to frame in the little slope-ceilinged space under the stairway for a junk closet. The addition would add just six hundred square feet of floor space, but after the tension of living in the bungalow, we were sure the expanded house would feel luxuriously roomy.

Again we buckled on tool belts, strung out extension cords, and set to work. We hired three carpenter friends to help us this time, but Kapa and I still did the lion's share of the work. I remember the long day when she and I wrestled the high rafters into place. After I nailed a fir branch to the ridge beam for good luck, we climbed down and walked into the orchard a fair distance to look up at our clean-framed roof. We grinned, whooped, and bear-hugged, hammers in our tool belts clanking together.

Once the new addition's roof had been sheathed, and the space was finally dried-in, we cut through the wall adjoining the old and new parts of the house and installed a passage door. We spent that winter working on the interior of the addition, framing closet walls, wiring in light switches and outlets, then Sheetrocking and painting. We still slept in the little loft in the original part of the house, but we'd had to remove the ladder to the loft because it was right where we put the new doorway into the addition. So each night at bedtime, Kapa and I went out that door, passed from the warmth and light and order of the familiar house into a cold, echoey, shadow-shot skeleton of a house, and we climbed, by flashlight, the squeaky, temporary treads of the new stairs. Then, through the little, low doorway that accessed the loft, we ducked back into the main house.

I think of the house as a portal between worlds: through the house I can go deeper and deeper into solitude, and from the house I can move further into community. Home is the hearth, a place of safety and centeredness, a microcosm, an enfoldment. But home is also the springboard for creative action in the world. In *The Poetics of Space,* the French phenomenologist Gaston Bachelard says this about the house: "First it is a coat of armor, then it extends *ad infinitum,* which amounts to saying that we live in alternate security and adventure. It is both cell and world." Sometimes the house leads inward into depths of solitude, and sometimes outward into wider and wider kinship. We go out into places more humanized and technologized, or into spaces more natural, more other-than-humanized. We dress up and head downtown, or we pack up and head for the hills, and home is how we translate between those different languages. To build one's own house is to extend our being into both worlds, and the more of the building we do ourselves, the more we interpenetrate with tools and ideas, neighbors and values, merchants and ethics, birds and ambitions, government and poetry, lumber, weather, curiosity, and bugs.

It's summer now, and I'm cutting into the kitchen cabinets with a Sawzall, a mean little tool especially useful for demolition. It doesn't cut neat, but it cuts anything. Although we have never quite completed building the house—closet doors aren't hung, baseboards aren't installed, there is a gaping hole in the mudroom wall where I once cut through to access the electrical panel—we are remodeling. I'm going to install a built-in dishwasher and add a little free-standing island opposite, with a countertop low enough for Kapa to comfortably knead her bread.

I've carved out one whole cabinet, a cabinet that, not so many years ago, I spent several days building. I don't like destroying my own handiwork this way, however mediocre it might have been, but such is the practice of home, doing whatever needs to be done over and over and over again. Kapa is forever digging up shrubs and perennials and moving them around in her gardens, trying to achieve elusive harmonies and contrasts. As a writer I get used to wholesale cutting and pasting of passages, as well as making endless micro-adjustments within sentences and phrases—performing the finish work on an essay. But the built-in fixtures of a house are not as easily rearranged as the paragraphs on a page.

Nevertheless, we have hired a cabinetmaker to build the island counter, which Kapa already calls her pastry table. It's due to be delivered next week, and so we've decided that this is the right time to also install a dishwasher. Of all the things Kapa and I quarrel about, nothing comes up more often than: Whose turn is it to do the dishes?! Several friends and a professional therapist have all suggested to us that installing a dishwasher might help us put that particular bugaboo to rest so that we can move on to more interesting territory. Kapa and I are both suspicious of technological answers to personal problems, but we are working longer hours at our jobs these days. So far we've managed it so that one of us is always home with Elliot, and we're trying everything to help us get through some of our domestic chores more easily. So I'm carving open the breast of the house and implanting a dishwasher, tooling the kitchen to relieve us for other tasks.

When I was a bachelor just starting to build this place back in 1984, my goal was to get a roof over my head as quickly as I could. I wanted to own my house outright, avoid paying rent or a mortgage. I didn't want to be trapped by debts in any particular job. As a writer, I accepted the likelihood that my income might always be modest. I loved working as a gardener, but I wanted my winters to write, and I wanted to be beholden to no one. I wanted to be free. So my strategy was to pay for necessities—and housing was the most costly of them—in advance. All I really needed, beyond food, clothing, and a roof over my computer, was solitude and plenty of time to think, study, and write.

What I got was somewhat different. In the process of building the house, friends lent me tools and volunteered to work beside me. Neighbors came by to watch or visit or help. Even strangers, emboldened perhaps by the nakedness of a house under construction, stopped in to introduce themselves and offer advice. The building inspector, whom I cultivated with courtesy so he wouldn't object to my use of nonstandard secondhand materials, became on his own a helpful counselor. The electrician failed to convert me to his Pentecostal religion, but by the time he gave up, he'd taught me the basics of wiring. All these people entered into what was supposed to have been a solo enterprise. They saw the very innards of my house, and I think they probably saw pretty deeply into me, as well.

What I'd overlooked in the beginning was that to build one's own house is to build it in an utterly specific place, a place with its own nature and culture. I might have started with a vacant lot, but I soon labored my way into community. I had no idea what interesting and generous people lived in my new neighborhood, how many of the older generation had themselves built these houses on my street. I set out to make a private dwelling for a hermit-writer, but I've turned to living among these folks as a husband-father-friend-citizen-neighbor.

I've got the cabinet carved open now, the old shelving dismantled, ready to receive the dishwasher. I've nicked the face frame of the remaining cabinet with the Sawzall—in fact, I've gouged it pretty badly. Kapa will have to try to match the color with touch-up putty. We divvy up chores these days according to our strengths: I pound most of the nails, Kapa does most of the sanding and varnishing. I try to slow down and pay more attention to the details; Kapa tries to relax her high expectations, make peace with funk. Houses and marriages both require maintenance and remodeling. If we're lucky, the house will keep working on us as much as we keep working on the house.

To Autumn

Where are the songs of Spring? Ay, where are they?
Think not of them, thou hast thy music, too—
—John Keats

Elliot, dressed in his fleecy, footed pajamas, climbs into his stroller. I wrap him up in a cat-hair-covered blanket so that just his face is showing, and buckle his seat belt. Now, trussed up snug as a papoose in a cradleboard, he peers out with raw curiosity. We are going on a little journey, an evening stroller ride, down the street to the pasture and back home, to put a soft edge on our busy day.

The autumn evening feels plush and mellow, a luscious fragrance thickening the breeze. There's fruit everywhere. Apples and pears litter the ground and more still cling to the branch. Our driveway is slippery with mashed apples, the road pocked with smooshed walnuts. In the garden, overripe tomatoes hang rain-cracked and rotting, broccoli stand gloved in gray aphis. Our whole place is messy and smelly with a gross, autumnal fecundity.

By day Elliot is a confident, even bossy, preschooler. He lords it over the kids who come to browse in our garden and orchard, to hunt on their knees for late strawberries, to stuff whole plums into their mouths, to gorge on ripe grapes till the juice runs down their cheeks. They even graze on leaves of fresh spinach, because it's sweet and nobody's telling them they have to eat it. All summer the boys have been picking green apples to use as hand grenades, and they even *eat* the green apples, that bitter tartness being something they seem to need. And Elliot is glad to share, but he's sometimes cocky with abundance.

Come evening, though, he goes strangely quiet and passive, as if he's topped out on fresh experiences and needs time to weave them into new meaning. Last night when we went for our evening stroller ride I had to carry him outside and buckle him in, slack, indifferent, heavy as stove wood. It aggravates me sometimes, how inert he can be, as if this threshold hour has hypnotized him. Maybe I am a little envious of him, safely undergoing some evening enchantment that I, in my active role as father-protector, must forego. By day, I've been feeling younger lately, delighted that being a father has restored a certain springiness, if not of body at least of mind. But come evening, I sometimes get swept into an autumnal mood, a sweet gloom, when all the responsibilities of being a father, a husband, a neighbor, and a wage earner seem woven together too tightly. I feel sometimes as if I'm living in some lovely and intricate tapestry, with colored threads binding every inch of my being. Then an evening stroller ride helps me breathe.

If the geography of our large yard is well mapped in Elliot's mind, the street is still a frontier, the beginning of territories unannexed to his domain. From beyond our mailbox, playmates and adventures beckon, but unknown dangers lurk, too. Crystal Lake Drive, our tree-lined street, is part of the commons, a convivial pathway connecting friends, but it's also charged with cautions and prohibitions. Nothing will draw an angry shout from Papa more quickly than Elliot's dashing into the street. Now, safe in his jammies, but leaving the fold of home, the street must seem to Elliot like unmastered country, wild, exotic, and unpredictable. He leans back in the stroller, eyes round as an owl's.

Our neighbor Jane is out in her backyard talking to her sheep. She has two Romney ewes, Beulah and Lulabelle, and has just this week brought home a ram, Fonsy, who tails the ladies around the small paddock. Fonsy is short and plump and, Jane tells us, prone to hoof rot. She paid fifty bucks for him, saving him from being auctioned off for cat food. When Jane, a childless spinner and weaver in her fifties, was diagnosed with cancer a few years ago, she realized that the one thing she'd always wanted to do was raise sheep, so she sold her house in Seattle and bought the rundown place next to ours. The first time I saw Fonsy, he had stationed himself in the farthest fence corner, looking chesty and ram-ish. Jane faced him, in barn boots, army coat, and watch cap, gripping a hoof pick in her hand, also looking dangerous.

"I don't have any business breeding them," she once told me. "Heck, I don't know how to deliver a lamb. I've had cats, but they never had kittens. If my goldfish ever had guppies, they must have eaten them before I noticed. Anyway, I know it's selfish, but I'm at the mercy of maternal instincts. I want lambs."

I know how she feels. Lately I've been wishing Kapa and I could have another baby. It may be just this blustery fall weather, but I want that vicarious languor and vertigo of pregnancy, the slow drama of gestation, the self-thinning enthrallment with a latent being. We would give the fetus a new name each month, "Tadpole," "Blue Moon," "Orangutan," and I would hum on Kapa's belly like a kazoo. We would carry each day as if it were an egg and the littlest things would make us cry. Kapa would be increasingly uncomfortable and sometimes sick, and I would be scared and attentive. Friends would call every day and ask how we're doing. Oh, Kapa and I agree that having just one child is enough for us, but sometimes we do get baby-happy.

Making love with the conscious desire to conceive a child must be the rarest moment in human sexuality. Nature's programmed us to just leap into the gene pool, without forethought or even foreplay, and with no bungee cords strapped to our ankles. If that one sperm in a million burrows into the egg, we'll figure out how to handle the consequences on the rebound. Kapa and I have friends who recently put aside their cervical thermometer, color-coded monthly calendar, and all the latex paraphernalia of contraceptive sex and took the plunge toward parenthood. They confessed to us that they felt a tinge of disappointment, under their genuine elation, when they conceived on the very first throw.

It's dangerous, I sometimes think, to deny the urge for a child. "Sooner murder an infant in its cradle than nurse unacted desires," declared Blake, double-bindingly. Desire is so invigorating, but it's also mercilessly complicating, sucking us into unforeseeable pleasures and predicaments. I don't know how I'd handle another child. I'm forty-six, Kapa's pushing forty. It still gives me a cold shiver to remember those infant nights when Elliot cried out so long and loud, when I'd carry him for hours, wailing in my arms.

Now Fonsy is trying to mount one of the ewes. He clambers onto her backside, but she bucks and twists away and Fonsy stumbles to his knees. Elliot chuckles quietly, chewing the fleece collar of his pajamas. We wave to Jane and stroller on.

Cars approach from both directions, and I steer the stroller into a driveway. There's a sudden pocket of warmer air here— it feels good, you could wear it, like smooth, old flannel.

"Hamburgers," Elliot says. And, yes, I can smell the grilling meat. Also the cloying fragrance of nicotiana. Farther up the street the acrid smell of ammonia tweaks my nose: Ray Lundberg's been delivering pickup loads of donkey manure to all the gardeners on the street this week. Now, from behind Ray's house, one of his jennies lets fly a warbling, excited heehaw and the other donkeys join in.

As the ruckus dies down, I hear the lowing of cattle from the auction yard a half mile west, and the roar of the Friday night football crowd at Parker Stadium. Sports announcer and stockyard auctioneer swap phrases back and forth in the same blurry, hypertrophied voice. When the breeze is from the north, the sky voice becomes a monotone growl, spewed from the throat of the fiberglass factory's extruder engines. Now a crow squawks overhead and I squawk back at him—three knuckle-throated epithets. Elliot looks up at me and grimaces, as if I'd said something embarrassing.

Will sounds and smells like these become the ground tones of Elliot's experience? Adults talking about lambs in a backyard, the pungence of fresh-sawn lumber, sparrows gossiping in a lilac, the stink of a faltering septic system, a curse for a car barreling by too fast? Can kids be imprinted on a landscape, like Konrad Lorenz's geese fixing on the first warm creature they meet?

I pick up a half-eaten apple from the grass. It's covered with yellow jackets, their bodies quivering with fierce energy. The apple pulses in my hand. Elliot stares impassively at it, as if gazing into a fire. Beneath the yellow jackets, I can see the clear impressions of a child's teeth. I'll bet I could take this apple around the neighborhood and find whose bite matches.

Claudia's dahlias are bent to the ground, hung over from Monday night's rain. The flowers remind me that I had promised to visit Leonard before the fall rains beat up his dahlia garden, but now it's too late. Leonard is a wry hermit, a lifelong bachelor lately retired from teaching university physics. When I told him I'd been reading about the worldwide decline in male sperm viability, his response was a gleeful, "Thank God!" Leonard is not known for his invocations of the Deity. Since my own reaction had been grief and dejection, Leonard's hosanna struck me as perverse. But, as he saw it, such an environmental catastrophe was the planet's roundabout way of reducing our species.

"A hell of a lot kinder than the plague," he argued. To him it was heartening evidence that nature was resourceful beyond our wildest systems-management dreams.

But then, Leonard does not have children. With no one to fend for but himself, he can glean more satisfaction from the prospect of our species' long overdue comeuppance. Delight in bitter irony is a pleasure with which I'm familiar, having made it one of the staples of my bachelor years. But it doesn't wear well with the mantle of parenting. I fervently hope that Elliot will be able to father a child someday if he so chooses.

I smell goat—rank, skunky, nose-tickling. Dorothy Jones must have borrowed a buck to service her does. Though I like strong organic odors, I wouldn't call this goat stink pleasant. But it is a wild and upstart antidote to sterility, to that urinal-cake sanitizing of the public aroma. Every spring I spade composted chicken manure into the flower beds at the county courthouse where I work as the gardener. The clerks and secretaries in their nice suits and dresses, squinch their noses as I turn that rich, dark fertilizer in. I've been assaulting their nostrils this way for twelve years now, and the flower beds grow lusher each summer. So they have all learned to say, "Ah, smells like a good year for pansies, Charles. Where *do* you get that stuff?"

"Yucko," Elliot says now. "What's that smell?"

"I think it's a buck, Elliot, a male goat. Do you dislike that smell?"

"Well, I kind of like it. It's just yucko, that's all."

Up ahead we spy Johnny and Beth, playing in their driveway. They see us coming and begin hollering, "Hi, Elliot!" Johnny is Elliot's age and his best friend. Beth, his sister, is eight. The three of them play together frequently, Beth accepting with ease the power and hassle of supervision. I invite them along. They are a-babble with Halloween plans. Beth's wearing pointy new witch shoes and launches into a description of the rest of her costume, spicing her narrative with screechy witch laughs. Johnny is practicing his pirate's swagger, slashing at roadside grass with a stick, shouting, "You scorby dog!"

Elliot, who runs wildly with these two friends by day, tonight slinks back in his blankie, almost wary. He hasn't said a word.

As we approach Bill-and-Judy's pasture, I see a family looking at the horses. Johnny and Beth run ahead. I don't recognize the people; perhaps they're newcomers to the neighborhood. The man is helping his toddler push carrots through the fence, and now I see that the woman is holding an infant. We all nod hello. The three horses shy nervously as Johnny and Beth thrust handfuls of grass through the fence. Elliot clambers out of the stroller and tumbles into the ditch, then scrambles up beside Johnny and puts his arm around him. I sidle over to the woman and peer down at her blanket-wrapped child.

"Oh, so new. May I see?"

Her flushed, hormonal smile says yes. I'm grateful that the distance American etiquette imposes between strangers may be suspended in the presence of an infant, that the chance to inhale a newborn's delicate cheesiness is given priority over personal space. The woman pulls the blanket back from a nubby, pink face.

"A boy?"

"Girl."

"And how old?"

"She's five days."

Oh, that milky smell. The hot doughiness of her cheeks. And what is the name for that scaly skin rash on her eyelids— blepharitis? All the intimate details of living with an infant— they seemed so indelible when Elliot was that small, but they are fading fast. I hear a voice inside say, "You'll never have another child," and I suddenly feel very old.

Beth wants a peek at the baby, and that brings the boys over, too, and we're a bit raucous now for the new mother, so I bow a thank you to her, and herd my charges back up the street. Elliot, after his brief flurry of activity, has retreated into silence, and I'm full of my own thoughts. At their driveway, Beth and Johnny shriek, "Good night!" and dash into their house. I pause in our front yard, drinking in the last rosy streamers of sunset, watching a hatch of insects cruise in a tight column above the grass, the swallows cutting and diving among them, twittering sociably. I can hear the burr of a distant lawnmower, Jane's sheep bleating, children shouting a few doors down—autumn's own music. A ragged string of crows flies over the house, heading for their roost by the river. Kapa looks out the kitchen window and waves to us, and we wave back as if we'd traveled far and been gone a long time.

Hut Dreams

I shuck off my tool belt, box up the lumber scraps, and step back to regard my new desk. It's a mongrel critter, cobbled together of pine boards, plywood, and a banged-up, mahogany-veneer closet door. One end of the desktop is held up by an oak filing cabinet, the other end rests on a ledger I screwed to the wall. Except for the half sheet of fir plywood, I've used nothing but scraps of lumber leftover from other projects.

This desk looks like it was born old, all its nicks and scratches suggesting a checkered past. The colors of its various woods shade from blond to honey to amber to chestnut, and the grains too are diverse: the grain of the fir veneer swirls like lines on a topographic map, while the straight, dark grain of the mahogany is fine as baby's hair. I like this desk very much. No one would ever, ever buy such a desk. It is not a commodity. It is barely a *thing*. I almost expect it to make intelligible noises.

With the desk finished, I can start moving my books and notebooks and files up here to this roomy, window-surrounded studio where Kapa does her painting and garden designing. My present study is downstairs, but that room is going to become Elliot's bedroom. Elliot and Kapa have just left to go grocery shopping, but this morning, while I was building this new desk upstairs, Elliot was downstairs building himself a house out of sofa cushions and blankets. As I traipsed back and forth through the living room carrying pieces of plywood and lumber, I heard him talking aloud inside his hideaway, doing different voices for various characters, making up the story of his little world. I imagine he was feeling safe and competent in that fantasy land because he got to say how things worked and how everyone behaved. And maybe, it occurred to me, that's part of the reason my desk is so important to me. My desk is a hermitage inside the house, a private little space where I go to try to make sense of the world. My desk is a hut whose walls are made of concentration.

I've told Kapa that I intend to use the move upstairs as an opportunity to organize my files, catch up on belated correspondence, and generally establish new habits of order and punctuality. It won't happen. Probably the opposite: I'll simply dump everything onto the spacious horizontal planes of the new desk and sink back as quickly as I can into the same old comfortable chaos. I don't know why, but I need a lot of disorder at my desk. Maybe disorder encourages my neurons to make connections. Maybe disorder pushes my brain toward making metaphors in order to stitch disparate things together. Or maybe all the books and piles of paper on my desk are like the tools and supplies, the dead machines and miscellaneous junk that fill all the shops and garages around the neighborhood, maybe they are the loose parts I need to make new stuff.

I roll my chair up to the desk and sit down. A desk may look like the seat of power and control, but it is also a portal into the unknown, into risk and confusion. Through the desk you can go anywhere, you can get lost. You would be well advised to unspool a thread behind you as you enter. Sometimes when you're writing, the flat surface of the desk becomes the molten present. Words sizzle and smoke as you squeeze them like lava from the pen. But as soon as they've cooled, you see that the new ground they've made is barren and inhospitable. So then you have to be weather, you have to pound the sentences with storms, you have to blow in spores and little bits of dead plant and animal. You have to make soil from scratch. You have to apply centuries of climate to each paragraph before it will grow anything. The desk is a kind of island you perform evolution on. So my desk, like Elliot's hut on the sofa, is a miniature world. If I am its master, that mastery is in service to the next interjection of mystery.

A bit of tidying up now, and I'll be ready to begin moving my stuff upstairs. I rub the mahogany with a dab of furniture oil, lay a pencil in the center of the bare wood, and go downstairs to get the vacuum cleaner. Our vacuum lives in the slope-ceilinged closet under the stairs where we also store the food dryer, bushels of potatoes, jars of jam, camping gear, suitcases . . . Packed overfull, it's one of those closets that gives you a slight sense of foreboding before you open it. I ease the door open a crack, watching out for my toes. When I reach inside and switch on the light, I find, to my great surprise, that the cubbyhole has been emptied out and claimed for a new purpose: the floor is padded with camping mattresses, pillows line the walls, and a dozen or more stuffed animals sit around the perimeter as if waiting for a guest of honor to arrive for a party. So I crawl inside.

I remember now that Elliot has been clambering in here recently to play among the pots and pans. Kapa must have cleaned it out for him, though where she put the potatoes and the vacuum I can't imagine. The closet is tucked under the slope of the stair, and the ceiling at its highest is no more than four feet. But I can sit upright and stretch out my legs, and the company's nice—two bears, two dogs, an alligator, a centipede, among others, and my own little stuffed turtle, Aphrodite. Beyond my tennies, the closet tapers down cave-like to just two feet in height, and extends way back under the stairs into darkness where only Christmas ornaments and college yearbooks reside.

When I was a child, I was always seeking out such hidden places, domesticating wild corners of our succession of houses. We moved often because my father, a talented writer, editor, and advertising designer afflicted with alcoholism, was always going on binges and losing jobs. I remember exploring each new rented house or apartment, claiming a secret place in an attic, in deep closets, behind dressers or desks. Because I was a boy, I called these places forts, or clubhouses, but they were really little huts or nests, places where I hid and dreamed. A whole house is too big and too complicated for a child to master. Scale is everything, and a closet is the perfect space for a kid to colonize.

When I walk down Crystal Lake Drive, I spy all kinds of huts in my neighbors' backyards: a big yurt, a little dome, miscellaneous outbuildings and wood shops, a couple of barns, a scatter of tents, camping trailers. There are ruins of an ancient treehouse in a cherry tree behind Myrtle's house, and a very elaborate, long-in-progress treehouse high in an oak in the Morton's backyard. The little hut in the Harrison's backyard, a steep-roofed and tall-windowed Gothic design, must have been their daughter Alice's playhouse. She starts college next year. And there are those garish plastic huts you can buy ready made from toy stores. Orange and blue extruded plastic, they are hideous to my eye, and I loathe the whole marketing mentality behind them, but kids like them, often better than Daddy-builts, precisely because they are so small.

Did my childhood love for secret spaces predispose me to build a house? Was a seed planted then that has grown into this dwelling? Maybe. But don't most kids love such intimate little places and spend a lot of energy creating them? Then why do so few kids grow up to build a house? Where does all that love and energy go? I was an unlikely candidate myself, with little exposure to tools or handiwork, an absent father, no close role models for creative manual labor. How did it come about that I find myself now in a closet in a house of my own making?

Last week I visited Elliot's kindergarten classroom, wearing my old leather tool belt crammed full of tools. After the teacher introduced me, I told the kids how I had built our house and showed them a few pictures. I let them heft my twenty-ounce hammer and feel how smooth the hickory handle had become with long use. I let them pull the removable shaft out of my screwdriver and change the blade from a standard slot head to a Phillips head. I showed them five kinds of nails and let them rub the rough surface of the galvanized sinkers, the smooth polish of the 8d finish. "You can do carpentry, too," I told them. "You don't have to do it for a living—although you certainly could. I know Alan's dad is a carpenter and you want to be one too, right, Alan? But you might also like building things for fun, or to make presents, or just for the pride of doing something challenging." I wouldn't try to pass myself off as a real carpenter down at the union hall, but the kindergarteners thought I was cool, and they all took turns squeezing the trigger on my twelve-volt drill.

Now I hear the back door open, and Elliot's little feet come galloping through the living room. "Papa!" he calls as he runs past the closet and up the stairs. "Papa! Papa?" Then I hear him say, "Oh!" and I know he's discovered my new desk, and I feel like jumping out of the closet and going up to receive his admiration. But now Kapa's coming into the house, clunking a bag of groceries onto the kitchen counter, and Elliot yells, "Kapa, come and find me!" I'll bet anything he's hidden himself under the new desk.

"Just a minute," Kapa calls, and puts something in the refrigerator. Now she's walking past the closet and climbing the stairs. My heart is pounding, but I keep still among the silent animals. How long, I wonder, will it take them to find me?

Altars to Hephaestus

"Hephaestus, the Smith-god . . . is ugly and ill-tempered,
but all his work is of matchless skill."
—Robert Graves, *The Greek Myths*

Sweating copper in my shop. The blue flame of the propane torch licks the pipe fitting and the metal blushes purple, ochre, and gold. When I touch the solder to the hot copper, the silver wire melts and quivers into the fitting. More solder drips off and solidifies in small pearls on the shop floor. The hiss of the torch, the acrid smell of the flux are as pleasing to me as the sounds and fragrances of cooking.

Now Elliot bustles in with an armload of toy trucks and, growling like a diesel engine, begins bulldozing the pile of sawdust under the table saw. He has a miniature workbench next to mine with its own array of hand tools, even a small leather tool belt his older cousins gave him for Christmas, and now, abandoning his trucks, he clamps a two-foot length of lath into his vise and nails on a shorter perpendicular piece—instant sword.

"Knave! Stand guard!" he barks, left hand on his hip, sword pointed at my heart. Then the copper pipe catches his eye, and he crowds up to my elbow. "What are you making?"

"I'm soldering a railing for your new loft bed. Watch."

I've cleaned, fluxed, and fitted another copper elbow to the pipe. Now I open the valve on the propane bottle and hold the spark tool to the nozzle. I know he's going to jump when the flame pops into life, and he does, dropping his sword. Playing the torch over the pipe, gradually heating up the copper, I sneak a glance at him: he's staring goggle-eyed, in thrall to the flame.

Hephaestus was regarded as a junior god on Olympus. He was so ugly his mother, Hera, disowned him. But what I love about Hephaestus is that he is the only god in the Greek pantheon who works, he's a blue-collar god with a real job. His services on Olympus are in great demand because he can fix anything, he has the touch. Tools and raw materials dance in his hands. He toys with silver and gold and makes them do tricks as if alive.

According to Homer, Hephaestus once fashioned three exquisite mechanical maidens to assist him at the forge, an ancient foray into robotics. But Hephaestus is not an industrialist. When he needs assistance, he doesn't build an assembly line, but three robot maidens. He has an erotic relationship with material objects.

Ugly, clubfooted, and clumsy of speech as he is, Hephaestus is married to Aphrodite, the goddess of desire, beauty, and love. Such a strange pairing! What were the Greeks intimating about the relationship between beauty and ugliness, desire and revulsion? Is the hidden connection between lovers forged in part by the material world? Are beloved objects essential to the bonds between the partners?

This at least may be asserted: the workshop is a place to go when things in the bedroom aren't working. And Hephaestus was a jealous husband, for good reason. Once, when Hephaestus learned that Aphrodite was planning a rendezvous with her paramour, Aries, Hephaestus exercised all his mechanical ingenuity to catch them in the act. Cunningly hiding a net under their trysting bed, Hephaestus gathered a bunch of other gods to witness the proof of his wife's faithlessness, but when the trap was sprung and Aries and Aphrodite dangled naked in the air, everyone laughed at Hephaestus, the cuckold, sputtering with impotent rage.

I close the valve on the torch and the flame expires with a pop. Now a fresh quiet coexists with the crackle of a fire in the tin woodstove. I move over to the stove and hold my cold hands up to the metal chimney. I'm a bit dizzy from the gas, and as I look about me, the shop swims a little.

What a restless place. The cheap table saw that dominates the center of the floor is littered with copper fittings, pipe cutters, coils of solder. On the wall above the workbench, saws, hammers, C clamps hang in disregard of their red-painted silhouettes. In the far corner cedar, fir, pine, oak, and maple lumber in varying lengths and dimensions lean together in a jumble against the wall. Two dozen cans of paint squat glumly on shelves beside the door. On the window sill agates, shards of obsidian, and the jawbone of a deer are all stitched together with spider silk. Despite the cobwebs and layers of dust, nothing feels settled in the shop, everything seems to strain toward its potential, as if each scrap of lumber, all the screws and nails, the scraps of metal under the workbench want to be reassembled into something a human would use, something lovable.

The shop is both museum and laboratory, a place for admiring things as the world made them, and for making the stuff of the world into new things. It's also a refuge and a playground, where I can revel in the music of screaming power tools, get greased up and filthy, fill my nose with the tang of sawdust and paint, even reel a little on the fumes of solvents. Sometimes it takes strong sensations to fire my synapses. The subtleties of nature don't always suffice.

I'm thinking about all the shops in the neighborhood, all the odd, impromptu spaces my friends have for their projects. My friend Sarah has a sophisticated little wood shop tucked in her garage where she fashions hardwood lamps. Her neighbor Joe has sheathed his back deck with blue tarps, a space where he builds displays for the local nature center. Jack and Elizabeth across the street from Sarah make elaborate wooden puzzles, their tiny garage tightly arranged with racks and racks of puzzles and sheets of plywood, and a little clean room for spray painting. Around the corner Louis has his glass-blowing shop, a ramshackle shed behind his house. Raymond builds recumbent bicycles in his carport. Matt, in the thick of renovating his fixer-upper, has the workshop set up in his living room, the doorways into the kitchen and hall draped off with flowered sheets.

If our town can host a yearly wine-and-cheese tour of local gardens, maybe our neighborhood should organize a beer-and-pretzels tour of workshops, sell tickets to benefit shop classes at the middle school, or to help a high school girl or boy become an apprentice electrician or plumber.

Fifty years from now history buffs will try to resurrect a neighborhood like ours for a living museum. But we don't feel like anachronisms. We feel like the dexterous hands of the body politic. We're the touchers and lovers of things. If the United States ever had a materialistic culture, a culture that valued things more than ideas, it does not now. Now we are idealists— we pay not for the thing, but for the advertised ideas of pleasure, convenience, efficiency. We regard things themselves as expendable, as mere vectors of sensations, unreal in themselves, only useful so long as they stimulate us, as if every object was pumped full of some cheap ether, and we snuffed it like nitrous oxide to get a rise out of it. Then the object is junk, an empty canister. We are degraded idealists, maybe just addicts.

Handicrafters, artists, machine toolers, manual tradespeople, do-it-yourself home owners—these are the ones who deserve the honorific "materialists," who love the heft and texture of things, who see and understand how one object connects to another, who apprehend both the reality and the potentiality of an object. They want to know the biography of an object, where it came from, how it was made.

If there are people who can communicate deeply with animals—chimpanzee confidants, dolphin trainers, horse whisperers—there are just as surely people who communicate with things. I'm lucky I live near a clutch of auto mechanics— Ned next door, Bob across the street, and Lex next to Bob.

They are all car whisperers. They divine messages from my car, truck, and lawn mower that I cannot perceive. These guys commune with internal combustion engines. When Lex clamps the stethoscope in his ears and leans over the engine of my Toyota pickup, I await his news with hope and expectation. I love my truck beyond its blue book value, and I know Lex understands.

Say it's your first day back to school, ninth grade. All day you keep hearing about the new shop teacher, how hairy he is.

At recess, playing hoops, you try to impress Frodie, your new flame, with some fancy dribbling, but she and her girlfriends are blatantly ignoring you.

You hear Frodie say, "He has hair growing out of his ears! It's so disgusting." But you can tell it's that kind of disgusting that girls are fascinated by, the kind of disgusting you hope to muster up sometime.

You don't care much about building bookcases and birdhouses, and there's only one tool you're interested in handling much lately, but you think maybe this shop teacher will be worth checking out, that something he has may rub off on you.

Seventh period. You take a stool at the workbench farthest away from him. He is ferociously ugly—scraggly blue-black hair and beard, a big wart over his left eye. One leg is a good four inches shorter than the other, so his shoulders tilt weirdly and his massive neck crooks up at a painful angle.

Now he writes his name on the board. The cursive flows from his hand and seems to move on the chalkboard like ripples on water—Mr. Godwin.

His voice is deep and ratchety. "Good morning," he growls, and you laugh a little, nervously, because it isn't morning, it's well into the afternoon. But that's all he says.

He has in one hand a thick bundle of copper wires a foot and a half long. Now he holds them up, showing them to each quarter of the room as a magician would. He begins to tease and bend the individual wires into loops and twists, one hand holding the bundle stock-still before him like a bouquet of posies, the other hand flitting about like a bird stitching an elaborate nest. From time to time his hand disappears into a vast pocket in his green shop coat, and bits of hardware appear, shiny steel hex nuts he weaves into the swirling circles of wire.

Then he turns his back to you and bends over his work. What's he doing? Is he breathing on it? Now he rotates slowly back around and you see it: standing on the bare ground of his palm, glowing amber as if in late sun, silhouetted against the dark sky of his black T-shirt, a huge, broad-headed tree spangled with silvery fruits.

All the girls sigh—elbows on the high shop benches, cheeks in their hands—and you notice all the other guys starting to fidget and look around for a clock.

Mr. Godwin is smiling lopsidedly, his wet black eyes staring off into some absent landscape. He is somebody you'd keep your distance from at a bus stop.

"Copper nut tree," he finally croaks. "Show you how tomorrow."

Light rain on the metal roof, a narcoleptic tintinnabulation. I'm groggy and grumpy after a midafternoon nap. I bumbled out here to the shop to try to wring some small accomplishment from the hind end of a wasted President's Day. With damp newspaper, wood shavings, and lumber ends, I kindle a fire in the woodstove. Sipping coffee I survey the unspeakable jumble of junk, toys, and tools strewn about the shop. Between projects the shop descends into a sort of purgatory for stuff, a limbo where each object awaits judgment—Save, Recycle, or Shitcan—before being returned to its rightful nail, bagged for Goodwill, or dumped in the trash.

I find my chair under boxes of Christmas ornaments and pull it close to the stove. Kapa has asked me to rip plywood for closet shelves, but I don't want to. I don't want to clean the shop. I don't want to do anything. The February funk, a parasite endemic to the rainy Pacific Northwest, has claimed another victim. Gusting rain rattles the windows like malicious applause. The woodstove smokes.

Now the rain thrums harder. The shop roof whangs and booms. It's as if I'm inside a drum—sound everywhere—the tools, the wood scraps, the paintbrushes, and steel wool are all just sound, one roaring cacophonous harmony.

Louder still, and it's my skull being drummed on, and I'm watching from someplace else. What I notice now: the broken-necked lamp on the wall, a splintered picture frame in the kindling box, a can of bent nails under the workbench. How sad and incomplete each solitary thing is. A bottomless silence beneath the hammering of the rain.

Can it be that the men—for they are mostly, though by no means exclusively, men—that I see in their garages, outbuildings, or utility rooms around my neighborhood, rebuilding carburetors, painting secondhand kitchen cabinets, cobbling together climbing structures for their kids, are servants of beauty and love? In a culture where so few things are cherished, spruced up, repaired when broken, rebuilt when worn out by steady use, are they sublimating the power of eros into the mending of material objects?

The rain has let up enough so that I can hear myself sigh. I pull a slip of paper out of my shirt pocket. It shows a rectangle drawn in Kapa's precise hand, labeled, CLOSET SHELVES— $57\frac{5}{16}'' \times 14'' \times \frac{3}{4}''$. She wants six of them.

Okay. Bike cart, outside. Bucket of ashes to the woodshed. Toys stacked in the little red wagon. Christmas ornaments to the loft. Wood scraps, sawdust, into the fire. I clear a place to work on the bench, put a fine-toothed blade on the circular saw. I still feel sluggish and inept, but I can do this simple task if I remember who I am.

The Fluid and the Concrete

Mid-August, midafternoon. The river is low, the shingle white with bleached stones. Baked air shimmers. The sun pulses through a high haze.

Lounging in the shade of a willow, I could doze, but I need to keep an eye on Elliot down at the water's edge. He's busy carrying potato-size stones to the inlet of a backwater pool, chunking each cobble carefully into place, building a dam. Along with the chime of stone on stone, I hear his chattering as he urges on imaginary cronies, "Pile it up here! Make it higher!"

He loves building dams, bulldozing roads in his sandbox at home, constructing forts of scrap lumber and old bedsheets. He's so wonderfully insouciant in his use of found materials, the world must seem like a magic cupboard, ever offering up the next perfect thing to make real his newest fantasy. As a child, I felt that urge to construct things, too. Though the world seems somewhat less tractable to me these days, that impulse has continued through the past fifteen years as I built our house.

Our house is just a ten-minute bike ride from here, and we've been coming to the river often this summer. We always start by skipping stones, looking for caddis fly larvae, or splashing each other. Then I leave Elliot to his construction work, and I retreat to my favorite spot under the willow, to let the river work on me. Gazing into the water, unhinged from thinking, I can sometimes feel my mind begin to float with the current, buoyant and calm. Thoughts swim through me shimmering like fish.

This quiet dreaming has competition, though: big diesel dump trucks growl along the far bank, hauling aggregate. Morse Bros. Sand and Gravel is over there—a vast warren of strip-mining pits, settling ponds, rock crushers, an asphalt plant, bulldozers with buckets the size of our living room. The concrete for our house's foundation came from Morse Bros. and the rock in the concrete came from the river.

Not so long ago the river was the main artery of transportation in the valley. For the first fifty years after Europeans displaced the native Kalapuya people from the area, almost everything and everybody traveled by steamboat, keelboat, barge, or canoe. Now that a web of roadways has been laid over the alluvial valley soils, and cars and trucks do most of the moving, we hurtle about in our personal vehicles oblivious of the river. Still, most of the rock for the roads came out of the river, from outfits such as Morse Bros. that quarry aggregate from the floodplain or dredge it from the riverbed itself.

Aggregate is what we call the whole, river-deposited mixture of cobbles, silt, and sand. After it's excavated, it gets sifted, sorted and washed. Much of the round rock is then run through a crusher to give it the sharp edges that make it stay put on a gravel road, or adhere better in the concrete used for building foundations and walls, sidewalks, bridges, and highways. Maybe we could better remember our debt to the river by making all bridges toll bridges—not to pay money, but to pay homage. At every bridge, we'd have to slow to a stop, pull a little pebble from the glove box, give it a kiss and toss it onto the lap of a statue of the river goddess. The statue would have a hole in her lap, and the pebbles would drop through the bridge onto a barge. Whenever the barge gets full, a tug boat hauls it back upstream, with a minimum of ceremony—maybe just a banjo player on top of the rock heap crooning Woody Guthrie tunes—and all the pebbles get returned to the river.

Elliot scrambles up to me with a hinged pair of white shells, the size of a cabbage moth.

"Look, Papa, a shell!"

"Oh, yeah. Do you remember who makes shells like this?"

"A freshwater mussel. And the Indians ate them, right?"

"And so could we, right?"

He lifts the tiny shell to his lips and pretends to gobble it, then hurries back to his dam-building. The Willamette right here is as wide as thirty elephants running shoulder to shoulder, a hurrying, extravagant migration, and as I look into the slick and swirling surface, the muscular surge of it unsettles me. Several years ago a young couple and their two small children were canoeing on the Willamette, just an easy paddle on a summer's afternoon. Suddenly, a floatplane practicing landings on the river came hurtling down on them, low to the water. The pilot never saw them, until the man and the woman had been struck by the propeller and thrown, dying, into the river. Their blood mingled with effluent from pulp mills and sewage treatment plants, with soil eroded from wheat fields, and oil from city parking lots. Some of the blood flowed out to sea, and some was consumed by algae and entered the river's food web. And the story, too, remains in the river, gets pumped onto the croplands and into our drinking water, imperceptibly reddening us.

In building our house, one of the few jobs I was afraid to do myself was pouring the foundation. From my limited experience working with concrete, I knew that if you made a mistake, you couldn't just take it apart and redo it like you could with two-by-fours. Where the mud set, there it stayed. So I got a bid from one of the bigger concrete contractors in town, and then another bid from a guy named Harold. I don't remember where I got his name from, but Harold told me he'd do the job for half the other bid, on the condition that I would serve as his laborer, help him build the forms and do the pour, and then, after the concrete had cured, strip the forms and load them onto his trailer. He said he could start the following week.

This arrangement appealed to me for a number of reasons: first, it was incredibly cheap. Harold, being a licensed contractor, could get a better price on the concrete than I could, and he was charging only a pittance for his labor, his know-how, his forms, and other materials. And second, I'd get to learn something about the art of pouring concrete from a man who exuded confidence in his abilities.

Harold must have been pushing fifty, just a hint of gray in his wavy, dark hair. With a chest like a racehorse and a punishing handshake, Harold was obviously used to giving orders and demanding respect. But I noticed that his eyes didn't quite meet mine when we spoke, and though he worked furiously, he seemed distracted. He had family problems, or his business was failing, or he'd always meant to go to Hollywood and now it was too late, I could only guess. But Harold was becoming a bitter man. "I don't know why I'm doing this," he said more than once, as if the size of my small house offended his masculinity, his sense of patriotic consumption.

Contractors, to save money, often put houses on the dinkiest foundations, barely a foot off the ground. Though I am thrifty to a fault and have splurged on almost nothing in building this house, I knew well who would be crawling under this house in the future to thaw frozen pipes, add a new wiring circuit, or drag out a recalcitrant kitty. I wanted a *high* foundation, twenty-four inches.

Harold was incredulous. "Look," he argued, "your house is going to be, what, seven hundred square feet? It's a shack. Don't waste good money on so much concrete."

I didn't mind buying the extra concrete, but I did suffer for my adamancy. Harold's forms for the foundation walls were half sheets of one-and-a-quarter-inch plywood. Each two-foot-by-eight-foot piece must have weighed at least forty pounds and was tricky to balance. It was all I could do to tip one piece onto my shoulder and shuffle to the building site. Harold slung *three* on his shoulder and tucked another under his free arm and walked through the mud as straight as Daniel Boone through the wilderness. He drove stakes with an eight-pound sledge faster than I could swing my twenty-ounce hammer. With me trailing ineptly behind, Harold formed up the footers and stem walls on a Thursday and Friday, and called in the concrete order. The pour would be Monday morning.

I was still exhausted when the concrete mixer arrived on Monday. I had a huge, oozing abrasion on my right shoulder from humping plywood, and a sore throat to boot. I remember the pour like a fever dream. I learned nothing about handling concrete except how to balance on one leg while extracting my rubber boot from the slime. I mostly raked muck and tried to stay out of Harold's way. When he climbed into his black Ford pickup late that evening, he told me, "Wait till Thursday to strip the forms. Hose them down, spray this oil on them, and load everything on the trailer. I'll pick it up at 8 a.m. Friday."

I went home to my rented room in town and straight to bed with a high fever. On Thursday morning I called Harold and croaked into the phone, "I'm sick. I can't strip the forms today. I'll try to get to it tomorrow."

"Never mind," Harold answered, "I'll do it myself. You weren't much help anyway."

Elliot and I are back at the river, making a little end-of-summer shrine on the beach. We've wedged a dozen round-shouldered stones upright in a ring, filled the center with clean sand, then arranged bits of shell, smooth twigs, and three big turkey vulture feathers we found along the path. Now Elliot scampers off to work on his dam, and I get comfortable under my willow.

Once, I know, the river was many-channeled, snag-filled and swamp-bordered—a vast riparian world where water and dry land commingled. Over the past one hundred and fifty years, the Willamette has been channeled and riprapped, diked and dammed. But the river is still a long, rich, sinuous *realm* running the length of its valley. With forests and farms and cities bordering it, the river keeps bringing water to our homes and wild animals into our midst. The fox sneaks into our backyards via the riverside. A beaver plugs the culvert, and the next rain floods the driveway. The osprey fly over, courting and crying. And what would our dreams be without the proximity of wild fish? Dry dreams, red-shifted and crusty.

Once the foundation was done and Harold was paid off and gone, I bolted the sill plates to the top of the walls and began framing the subfloor, cutting the rim joists and laying out two-by-eight floor joists on two-foot centers according to my blueprints. To my chagrin, the rim joist hung over the sill in the southwest corner a good four inches. I measured and re-measured my layout. Every time the tape measure said my floor framing was square. Why did it overhang the foundation? It took me a full day before I would even consider the obvious explanation. The foundation was out of square; the west wall was angled in four inches! Harold had screwed up.

It would have been perfectly within my rights to have demanded that he tear out that wall and build it back square. But I already had the floor framing in place, and I didn't want to wait on Harold to move ahead. In fact, I never wanted to see Harold again, but I tried to call him anyway, to tell him the problem and see what could be worked out. I got the operator; his phone was disconnected. I called a couple of lumberyards. Most of them didn't know Harold, and at the one where he had an account, nobody had seen him for a while or knew how to get in touch with him. So I put in a pressure-treated post to support the corner of the floor and forged ahead with framing the house.

Now I notice that Elliot is lying on his belly, peering intently into the water. I go and flop down beside him on the stones. Tiny fish—I count four, no, five of them—are penned in the little reservoir he's made. We watch them dart away from our prodding fingers, then stop and float so still they are almost indistinguishable from the glimmers of sunlight on the water. After a spell, I withdraw to the shade of my willow and sit gazing across the river at a stand of cottonwoods, leaves aflutter though there is hardly a breeze. The constant motion of the foliage is like sunlight sparkling on waves. It will dazzle me if I'm patient.

I think that concrete is more than just a sort of subservient stone. It is an ambiguous substance, a changeling. Wet, freshly mixed concrete is fluid, you can smooth it into the forms like cake batter into a pan. But once it's set, you can drive a truck on it. You can dredge a river for stones and use them to build a giant wall to hold back the river itself.

I can see just upstream from us the tall, concrete pump house, where the city's drinking water is sucked from the river. The pump house should be a shrine, too. Ugly pillbox though it is, it would deck out nicely in prayer flags and statuary, maybe some sinuous dragons carved from cedar logs by local chain-saw artists.

Elliot, plastered with mud, is still chattering orders to his cohorts, singing the praises of his monumental labors. Lost in my thoughts of the river, I've paid him little mind. But it seems that his game has changed—he is taking the dam apart now, throwing the stones up the shingle from where they came. And now he's wading in the pool, shouting, "Go on! Get out of here," herding the minnows toward the breach in his dam.

Choosing a Plot

Elliot is running among the gravestones, searching out vases of flowers that have been overturned by the wind. Whenever he finds a fallen bouquet, he sets it upright, fluffs the flowers, then hurries on to the next one. At age five, Elliot's in a phase where doing small chores, being in any way helpful, gives him intense pleasure. Arms flapping, he circles between monuments like some benevolent bird.

Sitting on my usual bench, I watch him flirt around the statue of the full-skirted angel. He throws a fir cone over the bluff, then flops to his knees to run his fingers over some cast-bronze deer antlers anchored in concrete. Here in the old part of the cemetery, big-leaf maples, garryana oaks, and Doug firs soar from the graves. Beyond the trees, four white exhaust plumes from the fiberglass factory rise like pillars of heaven. Behind me a forested slope falls steeply down to Crystal Lake, a debris-choked old oxbow of the Willamette River, filling up with silt, grass clippings, and rusty flower urns. From its watery recesses come the splashing and quacking of mallards.

The day has been bright and warm for November. But now as dusk approaches, the sun weakens, the ground, gravestones, and tree trunks begin giving up their heat. Chilly little breezes swirl by.

I am thinking about buying a plot here. The older part of the cemetery is what I'm drawn to, where the rows of leaning headstones leer like crooked teeth, and the ground undulates with a rhythm of rotting caskets. Several of the founders of Corvallis lie here, as well as the town's earliest African American residents. There's an impressive Civil War memorial—a fifteen-foot-tall Union soldier standing at parade rest—and one grave marker—a hollow iron obelisk—that bootleggers purportedly used for secret deliveries during Prohibition.

I'm not interested in a fancy gravestone for myself; my personal vanity is to wish for a big tree to root in my corpse. But the plots here are all filled, or sold and awaiting their owners. All I can purchase now is a plot in the featureless "South Lawn." Out there every marker must be flush to the ground to accommodate the lawn mower, and memorial plantings of, say, lilacs or a rose bush, not to mention an oak, are not allowed. It's even a boring place to throw the Frisbee. Elliot and I prefer this old section where there's shade, and where the gravestones raise challenging obstacles to throw around.

Flat grave markers may well be the death of cemeteries. How un-American of the mortuary industry to overlook the market value of standing monuments. Upright, ornamental tombstones are . . . advertising. In this age of "Pre-need Arrangements," funeral directors must be stunningly myopic not to see the allure of an old-style marble orchard, the way the stones beckon, "Rest here." You have to wonder what cultural insights future anthropologists will glean from those acres of gravestones, all those identical granite slabs bearing no religious trivia, no windy epitaphs, no record of military service or place of birth, no deer antlers, no engraved cherubs or angels to take rubbings of—nothing but names and dates. Out there on the South Lawn there's nothing but plebeian grass, and the roar of the grim reaper in the guise of a twelve-year-old-boy on a riding lawn mower.

A few rows over some fairy ring mushrooms are growing in loops through the grass. Earlier I noticed some shaggy manes by the mausoleum. We'll pick a few on our way home and sauté them with scrambled eggs for supper. To either side of me a line of tall, craggy-crowned Douglas fir trees stand along the top of the bluff. Some are broken topped, all are mangy with lichens. In the slight breeze they lean, twist, and creak. These trees are a hundred and fifty years old, stirringly beautiful in their weather-beaten profiles, and full of heart rot. They've survived seven generations of lumbermen by their proximity to the dead, a magic I'm flirting with here today.

One kind of plot is a rectangle of bare earth. But plot can also mean the sinews of a story. I can shop for a plot here in the cemetery, then go home and work out the plot of a novel. This evening Elliot and I will play pirates and plot to capture Kapa as she transplants lavender to a sandy plot in the herb garden. If I can plot a story, deliberately arrange and emphasize its events to reveal their dramatic and emotional significance, how much can I shape the plot of my own life? As much as I try to be deliberate in how I use my time, it still seems like my days roll past in a plotless swirl, its moments sometimes vivid but often blurred. My life, as every one's life, has all the stuff of a good story—conflict, drama, pithy dialogue—but it's hard to know what it *means,* because after all I'm not separate from my life, I'm not in a position to weigh it and say how it's shaped. I'm immersed in my own story as a fish is immersed in its stream. I can choose my values, I can choose my friends, I can choose to stay put and make a home in this neighborhood come what may, but I can't control what will happen next. That plot is not for the choosing.

On other visits, Elliot and I have traced with our fingers the names incised on the gravestones.

"What's this name?" he asks.

"Thomas John Morton."

"What's this name?"

"Beulah T. Adams."

He can be tireless in this game. I'm always the first to quit.

One day last month we traced our way into the farthest corner, where we wound up touching the letters of the last marker, a flat stone hardly bigger than a brick.

"What's this name?"

"Baby," I said.

Elliot cocked his chin up at me, his eyebrows stitched and the corners of his mouth turned down.

"What?" He stared at me, waiting for more.

"The stone only says 'Baby.'"

"So, was that its name?"

"No, I don't think so. A hundred years ago it was pretty common for a child to die soon after it was born—life was tougher, and medicine wasn't so good—and sometimes parents would not name their child until they were sure it would live."

"Why wouldn't they give it a name?"

"I'm not sure. Maybe the parents could feel a little less sad if they pretended their baby had never left God. Would that make sense?"

He squinched his eyes a little tighter and looked down at the stone for a moment. Then without replying he walked away.

Last week I was sitting in a little-kid chair, knees almost to my nose, in the local elementary school library listening to the city traffic engineer explain the options for widening our street. Besides two standard twelve-foot travel lanes, we were offered a menu of amenities: bike lanes, sidewalks at the curb, sidewalks separated from the curb by a planting strip. None of us who live in the neighborhood wanted Crystal Lake Drive widened at all, but that was not an option.

"When the traffic gets heavy," the engineer warned us, "you may change your minds."

My tiny chair was giving me sciatica, so I stood in the back for a while. There on the wall were a set of crayon drawings by second graders, each one titled, "My House." Several pictured boxy apartment buildings, one showed a travel trailer hitched to a car, another, impishly, a treehouse. Most, however, were two-dimensional front views of two-story gable-roofed houses, a door in the center and a window on each side, rather like the mouth and eyes of a friendly face. In reality, there are only a couple of such houses in our neighborhood. Our streets are lined with cheaply built ranch-style houses interspersed with apartment complexes, all knocked up during the housing boom of the early seventies, but no such buildings appeared in any of the pictures on the wall. These drawings, I was thinking, must be storybook houses, "normal" houses, the houses all these children wished they lived in.

But one drawing was different. It, too, was a two-story house, but it had been drawn with some rudiments of perspective—a three-dimensional dormer jutted from the roof, a front porch leaned into the yard. The roof was scribbled over with slashes of red, and from the upstairs window a stick-figure child with hair in flames was screaming for help. Whether this was the child's recurring nightmare, or a record of a real tragedy, or, scariest, a signal of an abusive home life, what brought me nearly to tears was the realization that this child alone among his or her classmates showed a grasp of perspective, as if early hurts, fears, and losses had already broken the relative wholeness and innocence this child should be immersed in, and initiated the fractured consciousness of a wounded world.

"See!" I wanted to cry to the traffic engineer. "We don't want our street widened, our neighborhood torn by more cars. We want relief from the endless assault of progress on our homes." Since Kapa and I sit through a lot of such meetings these days, make a lot of phone calls, write a lot of letters to the editor, I'm always looking for nearby wild places where I can walk off my anxiety, reboot my senses, cool my brain. I like to tunnel through rabbit thickets in vacant lots, besiege kids in their backyard tree forts, or just sit and sulk in a certain ivy-grown ravine. There are exotic and strange places in the neighborhood, and power spots abound, if I'm satisfied with modest amperage.

This cemetery is howling with energy. My loudest desires trail off into whispers here. Thoreau, on his rambles around Concord, tried out the ownership of every farm. I try on possible graves.

Dusk now. Almost time to call Elliot in and head for home.

There are wispy streamers of mist floating above the ground, long and slender as parade dragons. Then, quite suddenly, the whole cemetery is blanketed waist deep in gauzy ground fog. The rapidity of the fog's condensation is uncanny. But now that it's arrived, the fog feels substantial, and somehow animal-like, possessed of mind and appetite. It is very white and dense, thickest at the top, thinning near the ground. I feel as if I'm looking down on a cloud, and I guess I am.

Elliot is entirely within the fog, but he seems to be unaware of it as he tilts around a berry-laden holly tree in the farthest corner. The fog is still rising, like water filling a tub. I stand on tiptoe to keep an eye on him. Overhead, the faltering sky's gone to cold blue silk. Jupiter burns close to a slender, bone-white moon. The fog seems to be working like a lens, gathering the last light from the sky and magnifying it earthward. Beads of moisture on every grass blade glow, creating a pointillist sheen.

I shut my eyes. I can hear a very pale rustling—vapors rising from the lawn—and feel the fog beading minutely in my beard. When I open my eyes, evening has settled in. The ground fog has risen to meet descending shadows. I shout to Elliot and he banks and flies my way.

Maybe this grave shopping is just a game, a flirtation with some imagined postmortem existence. Maybe, when my terminal illness arrives and I'm *really* facing last things, I'll realize that all these forays to the cemetery were just diversions, just misty folderol. What am I after here anyway? Am I trying to communicate with the dead? No, the real question is, can I communicate with the living? Of course I communicate with the dead! I'm *made* of the dead. I'm splayfooted just the way my daddy was, and when I cough, I hear him cough in that exact same key. Try and *not* communicate with the dead! Try to get absolutely quiet. When I attend my thoughts I hear more voices than I'm made of. There's a crowd inside, not all coeval with my time on earth.

The capacity for the forethought of death is supposed to be one of our human species' defining peculiarities, an ennobling burden that elevates us closer to the gods. I doubt it. I believe that the awareness of the ever presence of death is a given of animal existence. Our human oddity is to have a mind so prestidigitatory as to be able to *forget* death, to hide our mortality under shells of ideas, to act boneheadedly as if we were free from death, and to be shocked and outraged when death finally latches onto us. I am by no means an exception, but I hope that maybe hanging out in this lovely cemetery with a small, bodacious child for company will help me keep my own death lightly in mind. Then choosing a plot is simply homework.

A week ago Elliot and I were throwing a Frisbee in the old part of the cemetery. He hasn't learned to catch yet—he ducks away from the disk if it comes near him—but he throws pretty well. We were standing twenty feet apart in an avenue of granite monuments, most of them waist high to Elliot, but a few as tall as a grown man. The tombstones defined an impromptu Frisbee court, encouraging accuracy. We threw straight and flat, aiming for each other's gut.

Not infrequently, though, a wayward toss thudded into a gravestone. Each time Elliot cracked up. The sudden interruption of flight struck him as hilarious, and I got caught up in the slapstick, too, laughing along until my belly was sore.

Then he wound up and flung one way over my head. I turned and dashed after it, leaped over a low headstone and snared the Frisbee in the next row.

Elliot clapped and yelled, "Good catch, Dad!"

I leaned on a stone to catch my breath, pulse pounding in my ears. Forty-six years old. Bum knees, trick back. Standing with a purple Frisbee on a freshly dug grave.

Grass Man

When I was ten years old, not much taller than the handle of the lawn mower, my father taught me to mow. "Watch your feet," he told me, "and go slow until you get the hang of it." He placed his blue canvas boat shoe on the deck of the mower, bent over, and wrapped his long white fingers around the rope handle. Once, twice, three times he pulled the starter, but each time the engine coughed to a halt. I felt like shoving him aside and yanking the rope myself, so eager was I to run my first dangerous machine. On the fourth pull the mower roared to life and I raced off almost before the rope had recoiled. Pretending not to hear my father's continuing admonitions, I plunged headlong across the lawn and into the cult of the internal combustion engine.

I knew that my father was planning to retreat to our glassed-in side porch to listen to the St. Louis Cardinals on the radio, and to drink his Saturday's first bourbon and water. As much as I loved to listen to baseball, I didn't care. This was better. This was an entry into a wider world, a world of power. Even the offer of payment—a whopping whole dollar he'd promised me if I finished the entire yard—was less important than getting to run that exhilarating machine. It pulled adrenaline from my glands as steadily as the Briggs & Stratton sucked gas through the carburetor.

In twenty-five years as a professional gardener, I have mowed more acres of grass than a herd of Jerseys. I've driven a diesel tractor pulling a twelve-foot gang mower for whole days over hills of empty parkland, backed brush hogs into blackberry thickets tall as a house, and ridden a nifty little triplex reel mower—the kind they mow golf course greens with—over the lawns surrounding the county courthouse. Over the years my infatuation with the machinery of mowing has shriveled, while my respect for the grass itself has flourished. Grass and I are in deep cahoots, and I have to confess, I am a grass man. I love the plush look of a green lawn, the cush of grass underfoot. I love to smell it, touch it, sleep on it, make love on it. I like to lay on my belly in tall grass and watch insects climb through an architecture more intricate, more spired and cantilevered, more electric with predators and pitfalls than any celluloid space station. I like to play foolish music with a blade of grass till my lips tingle, then floss my teeth. I like to tickle my son's ear with a grass spear. I like to suck the smidgen of sap from a stem.

And I love the megaflora grasses even more. Kapa and I planted a clump of black bamboo outside our bedroom window and the stalks rustle like petticoats all night, toss calligraphic shadows on our ceiling at dawn. I'm a connoisseur of corn on the cob, and nutritionally dependent on wheat, rice, and oats—grasses all. (Sugarcane, too.) I love grasses large and small, structural or edible, tuneful, whispery or mute. They say Lillie Langtry loved to roll naked in the morning dew, and so do I. But these days, I hate to mow.

Here I am, though, jouncing around our rutted backyard on the little red riding mower, decapitating the grass. The smelly tractor and I are what centaurs have devolved to, a sad confabulation of man and machine, dedicated, not to anything magical or sexy, but to barbering the lawn. I wince with each bounce, my spinal discs banging together like freight cars. Down by the gear shift my sciatic nerve twitches in its ham.

The late summer day, sunny and clear, is lovely—at least, out there it is, beyond my immediate atmosphere of clamor and chaff. My nose and eyes weep doggily. The noise is omnivorous, it gobbles up the scoldings of scrub jays, the alarms of the crickets, the bright cries of Elliot and his best friend Johnny, waving to me from high in the apple tree. I sit up straight and salute them, sensing how they envy me. Eight-year-olds, they would mow in a minute. They would hybridize happily into boy-machines. The cartoons and comics they devour are full of such bionic heroes.

Our neighbor Jane's four Romney ewes stare at me through the wire fence. Their half acre of grass is browsed to the quick, so the smell of all this fresh hay, so close, so fragrant, and all going to waste makes their hair curl. Kapa and I have considered grazing sheep, too. Moderate grazing often favors the grass: the close clipping stimulates branching and fanning of blades, producing a denser, sturdier turf that resists invasion by woody species. But there are hassles galore in keeping livestock, starting with fences and ending with slaughter, and anyway, we don't really want to turn our grass into wool, or meat. Grass unto grass, we say, but therein lies a challenge.

Kapa and I have a small orchard, a huge garden, grapes, blueberries, persimmons, you name it, and we manage to overwork ourselves gardening less than half of our acre. On the other half, we grow grass. But without maintenance of some kind—mowing or grazing or controlling weeds with herbicides—the grass would be overtaken by shrubs and tree seedlings.

Chances are that this little swatch of ground, like much of the Willamette Valley, has been sprouting grass happily for ten thousand years. When the first Europeans—trappers and explorers, then missionaries and farmers—arrived here less than two hundred years ago, they found the valley landscape dominated by open grasslands: wet prairie in the low areas where water stood in winter, dry prairie on the better-drained uplands. Oak forest held some of the hilly ground, and ash trees grew thick along the watercourses, but mostly the valley was grass—vast prairies of blue gramma, red fescue, tufted hair grass, and nodding bent.

It took work to keep it that way. Our predecessors, the Kalapuya peoples of the valley, had their own set of reasons to favor grassy prairie—easier traveling, better browse for deer and other game animals, more convenient gathering of staple foods like camas, tarweed, and acorns. Perhaps, too, they enjoyed a sense of spaciousness. They didn't plow or mow or keep domestic cattle, but they did maintain most of the valley in an unforested state for ten millennia or so with one powerful tool: fire. Every fall, after the season's herbage browned out, the Kalapuya torched the prairie, burning much of the valley from today's Eugene to Portland.

When David Douglas, the plucky Scots botanist who gave his name to the Douglas fir tree, rode through the Willamette Valley in 1828, he complained to his journal again and again about the scorched landscape. "Country undulating; soil rich, light, with beautiful solitary oaks and pines interspersed through it . . . but . . . all burned and not a single blade of grass except on the margins of rivulets to be seen." I haven't been able to find any historical descriptions of the Kalapuya in the act of torching those autumn prairies, but it must have been quite a sight: the fire-starters, carrying torches of pitchy fir, loping out along the margins of the meadows, maybe ululating a song to the wind and the fire, to the grasses and the game, while the children and the elders encamp on top of Bald Hill to watch the hanks of smoke rising and braiding together into heavy gray ropes, the serpents of fire slithering along before the wind.

Elliot and I, on a hike through Finley Wildlife Refuge, watch from a hilltop as a convoy of huge combines swath across mile-wide fields down on the valley floor. Crows and turkey vultures flock to the small carrion left in their wake.

Out of the blue, Elliot asks, "Did buffalo used to live in the valley?"

"I don't think so. There's a herd of elk here in the refuge, though."

"How old do you have to be to drive a combine?"

"Fourteen and three-quarters."

"Nah!"

"Really. I'll bet you some of the boys running those combines don't have a driver's license yet. I drove a combine when I was fourteen and three-quarters."

Across the valley, a giant column of smoke burls into the sky and flattens out into a bruise-colored cloud. After trucking the grain away, the farmers often burn their straw to rid the soil of fungus and diseases, torching the stubble with tractor-pulled flamethrowers. Ninety percent of the world's commercially grown grass seed—rye, fescue, clover, orchard grass—is produced in the Willamette Valley. It's exported around the globe, for lawns in Alaska, golf courses in Kuala Lumpur, pasture in the ashes of the Bolivian rain forest. Grass seed is one of the staple crops of our regional agriculture. We are a people fattened on grass.

It's possible that we are also flattened by our grass, that the homogeneity of our suburban lawns announces the narrowness of our relationship to nature. Do the demographics of grass express a preference for the uniform and the plain? Does the lawn serve as just a slavish foreground to the house, it's horizontal plainness accentuating the building's vertical angles and ornament? Snooty neighborhoods can be tyrannical about grass—let yours get weedy or tall, let it brown out unwatered in July, and you will feel the heat from your neighbors.

A few years ago, Kapa and I considered torching our backyard. Fire, we knew, was the finest tool for maintaining a landscape in grass, but burning our lawn would have raised eyebrows among the neighbors. So we decided to resign from the lawn-scape and go prairie.

"We'll just let it grow!" we said, delighted by our audacity.

And it was beautiful. Beyond the persimmon tree began something like a native place, the grasses stretching taller and taller. We ogled the graceful weave of subtly hued colors, the seed heads waving in the evening breeze. It was easy to credit reports of the munificence of the aboriginal prairies, of horses wading to the shoulder in a sea of grass. Elliot and his friends loved to make tunnels through the arching grain, to creep and spy on Kapa and me working in the garden. They'd pop up and holler, "Woo-hoo!" and duck down and giggle hysterically.

It seemed there were more good insects around that summer, and more swallows and bats, too. Why did we ever mow?

Then came the letter from the fire marshal, polite but emphatic. It said, in effect, all grass will be mowed to a height no greater than eight inches after the first of July. Comply, comply, comply. The clerk I phoned at the fire department pleasantly told me that the ordinance was cut-and-dried—either mow, or the city would mow for us and send us the bill.

It was a small grief, but we went through all the classic stages—anger, denial, begrudging acceptance. Still, we hemmed and hawed. A day of heavy showers reduced the potential for fire, and we didn't think the city would press its ordinance in the absence of real danger. Then another hard rain dragged down much of the grass, and the prairie began to look kind of ragged. The kids quit hiding in the flattened grass, preferring to kick the soccer ball in the neighbor's neatly clipped side yard.

The final straw came in late July, after hot dry weather had returned, and the parched grasses, in full-headed ripeness, lifted up and waved once again in a late evening breeze. Resigned to the mowing, I rented a tractor and brush hog. With the tractor idling, I took one last loving stroll through the rustling prairie, admired the delicate sweeps of color—the pale ochres, siennas, and rusts—stroked a few of the swollen seed heads. Then I noticed a knee-high Nootka rose bush sprawling amid the grasses, and then another, and another, and here and there stout clumps of Himalayan blackberry, and lots of vicious little hawthorn trees!

It was natural succession, and it was taking over our backyard! Succession, not into a picturesque natural woodland, not into maples or oaks, or even Doug firs—no, a thicket of thorns and brambles was sprouting up under my feet! For the first time I felt that diesel tractor idling behind me as, not an evil implement, but a trusty ally. I mowed with new purpose, the beautiful grasses just collateral casualties in a battle against nature barbed and shameless.

Last mow of the season, chopping down the brown stubble before the autumn rains begin—which will happen tomorrow, according to the weatherman. A fleet of battleship-gray clouds steams past Marys Peak, ominously punctual.

Elliot's riding in my lap, steering. He is simply awestruck by the mower's eleven horsepower, so proud of this borrowed force that he's oversteering, weaving back and forth in his ardor to master it. His spirit's prancing. Shivers run over him as if the glory of the moment is shaking him with a glad fever.

My spirit's conflicted, caught in the intersection between grass and gasoline. I want to help Elliot answer the demands of the world, but what if some of those demands are misleading and unsustainable? I hope he outgrows his fascination with machines faster than the grass overtakes our streets when the gas is gone. At Elliot's school the other day, I heard the counselor use a deft phrase, telling the mother of a disruptive child, "I believe you've overempowered him." And I thought, yeah, we're an overempowered culture, aren't we? If this mower ride is a sort of initiation for Elliot, it's a bogus one, an initiation into a sham society of ill-spent power. I hug him close, for safety's sake or in fatherly foreboding, and nudge back on the throttle.

I long for a more animal, less mechanical relationship with grass. Yet at the same time, I see how excited Elliot is, so inspired by his deeds that he trembles with energy, humming snatches of "Yankee Doodle," bouncing in my lap. He loves me for giving him this opportunity, this trust, this enormous power. I'll be his hero at least until supper.

Live grass is green fire, a cool combustion, sunlight slow-cooking carbon and spice into shoots and roots. I kiss Elliot on the cheek, he climbs down, and I grind the transmission into a higher gear. Gotta get this job done in time to make supper. The swallows are out, zinging through the air all around me, snatching the bugs stirred up by the mower. My back aches and my hands smell of gas, reminding me of William Burrough's spooky name for our age, the "gasoline crack of history." In my fatigue I'm treated to one of those wild flashes of spurious omniscience: as if from high above, I see myself grazing along with all the herbivores throughout the ages, a little glint of metal and flesh moving like a beast over a field of green.

Night Canoe

Our plan is to paddle to the center of the lake and drift there until full dark. We want to lie in the bottom of the canoe and star-bathe. The evening chill and the encroaching darkness are rousting my senses from postsupper drowsiness. There are frog smells, stone smells, aromas of drowned weeds. There are sounds that could be birds rising or stones falling.

Kapa turns in her seat. "Let's go as far as the beaver lodge." I swing the canoe about and we paddle into the reflection of South Sister. Hosmer Lake is odd-shaped—two small roundish lakes joined by a bulrush-lined channel. We head quietly into that channel, detouring through mats of pondweed.

We stroke the water in unison, silent enough that when we spot a V-wake ahead and drift to a near stop, the wake continues coming straight toward us, gradually resolving into a mother pintail with five ducklings in tow. They pass within a foot of our bow, clucking softly. I had not known we were invisible, but the sudden realization causes a surge of tenderness in me. My arms and legs feel distant, and stiff as tree limbs. I want to be climbed, nested in. Transfiguration seems possible, even imminent. Then, from the rushes, a couple of coots laugh. The pintail family flaps away, as if they'd smelled alligators.

The darkness grows. I can barely see the channel. The Milky Way, thick as frog spawn, would be easier to follow. I ask Kapa if we should turn back but she whispers that she wants to go as far as the otters. Again, we swing about. Higher magnitude stars bob beside us in our little bow wake. The channel is only discernible as a glossy blackness. South Sister looms under the Pole Star. I rudder the canoe according to my wavering memory of which way the channel winds next.

We come out into the north lake. Near here is where we saw the otters yesterday. We'd been on foot, skirting the water, following the dry hummocks covered with blueberry bushes, occasionally jumping a small slough or squishing across a reedy, wet stretch. It was late afternoon, not much stirring except the redwing blackbirds. We had just crossed a derelict footbridge when we heard sizable rustlings from a patch of reeds, then splashings. We'd come upon a backwater pool full of lily pads. Suddenly a blocky gray head, whiskered like a small walrus, popped out of the water, and then another surfaced. Otters. Grunting and hissing. They cussed us roundly, then dove and disappeared out a narrow channel connecting to the lake, followed closely by two of their young.

Tonight, we drift in darkness and silence. Stars swirl overhead. I notice my breath coming and going. From time to time a small fish jumps somewhere nearby.

It has occurred to me, other times in deep quiet, that the small sounds I hear—a rustle of leaves, a far dog—originate neither inside nor outside my head, and are not a commerce between a hearing subject and an object heard, but spontaneous little tears in the fabric of silence. My ears, my life, are unsunderably married to those sounds.

Listen for the fish to splash. . . . That brittle, ringing overtone.

I'm straining to see movement along the shore. I actually believe that if we wait patiently enough, the otters will swim out toward us. The canoe is rooted in pondweed. The water buoys us. If Elliot were along on this trip, he'd be getting restless by now. Silence, and things that come into silence, shy away from small children.

My mother was never much of a camper, but I suddenly think of her, wish she was here. A few summers before she died we drove to a lake one Sunday and rented a tiny sailboat, one of our precious few adult outings together. We tootled up and down the lake, Mom lounging in the bow in her dowdy-skirted black swimsuit, me at the tiller in loud Hawaiian baggies. I steered us into a bay out of the wind for a quick swim. "Don't touch the rope," I told her. "You'll just drift right here." I bailed out into deep water. When I surfaced, the Sunfish was already twenty yards away under full sail. Mom was at the tiller, the jib rope in her hand and her face full of good-bye. I don't know whether she thought she was going to drown, or me. I must have swum a mile before I caught her. After a while we could laugh.

The night chills down. I am suddenly shivering. If I unzip the knapsack to get my down vest, the quiet will be undone, the moment broken. One of the smaller griefs is to be forsaken by otters.

I am on the verge of giving up when Kapa speaks. "I'm ready to go back." She isn't whispering. There's no pretense of stealth. The otters aren't coming. Suddenly I'm tired, ready to lie in the bottom of the canoe, drink in the Milky Way, and drift off.

Somehow the channel is easier to see in this direction. We slip along briskly, like a couple of teenagers headed for the drive-in. Kapa points her paddle up ahead: a heron, huge and ghostly green, almost phosphorescent, hoists itself from the shallows and flies obliquely toward the open lake. If there was a moon, it would gape.

Then, out of nowhere: "Wh-whack! Wh-whack!"

Beavers.

Tail-slaps start raining down like mortar rounds, unnerving. We can't see them, only spumes of spray where they splash. There must be three of them at least, maybe five.

Crack of beaver tail whacking the water: violent. I think I see a shape moving to my left, then—whack!—a salvo lands behind me to the right. The sound, though crackling at the edges, has at center a dull, thudding wump, like an exploding cabbage, or a jaw or nose. After a few abusive minutes of this, we dig our paddles into the lake and move out of range.

Too late, I remember the flashlights, stowed in the knap-sacks specifically for spotting beavers. I toy with the idea of paddling back, but frankly, I'd sooner knock on the door of drunk neighbors quarreling.

When I see silvery bumps coming up the channel trailing wakes, I imagine I am finally spotting the beavers. But Kapa has already shipped her paddle and gone into a trance. I swing the flashlight across the water. Otters—four of them—swim northward off our starboard bow. When they come abreast of us, just ten yards away, the two adults pop up out of the water onto a downed tree trunk and begin to beat their heavy tails on the log, sniff each others' butts, and scramble over one another. Then the pups slip up onto the log, too, and they all scurry back and forth, over and under one another as slick as seals.

The adults still stop to pound tail now and again, and as we drift closer—Kapa could touch them with her paddle—I begin to sense that these otters are, in a word, freaked. My best guess is that they are frazzling out between intense curiosity and abject fear. Imagine what a flashlight must look like to an otter. Blinding. Stupefying. A brilliant hole in the night. I'm nearly certain that they have no sense of being themselves illu-minated, and I'm not sure if they know there are other mam-mals behind the light. It's possible that they've seen flashlights before and are less agitated than I imagine. But I begin to feel cheap, exploitive. From behind my one-way window, I am see-ing the otters stripped. I douse the light.

We have seen the otters. I feel blessed, indeed, but also a tad sullied. The night, up until the end, has been full of recip-rocal visitations. The swallows gleaned insects in our wake.

The trout altered their courses as our shadow sailed over them. The heron knew we were coming before we knew it was standing. And the beavers, well, beavers will inherit the earth. Only the otters got seen without getting to see.

We paddle out into the center of the lake, unroll foam pads in the bottom of the canoe, and stretch out under the gunwales, cheek to cheek, Kapa with her feet in the bow and mine in the stern. A shooting star zips through Pegasus. I feel warm air at my nostrils that must be breath Kapa has just exhaled. We lie in our jackets and down vests, exposed to the heavens, bottomlessly in love, seeing stars beyond believing.

Crow on the Roof

From up here on the roof, I can see the frumpy profile of the Coast Range to the west, columns of factory smoke rising in the north, neighbors' houses all around. It's about 7:30 a.m., a little early on a Saturday morning to start making a big ruckus, so I sit on the ridge and sip my coffee, watching three crows wrangle over a dead possum down in the street, and carefully thinking through this stupid roof project, berating myself for not getting it right the first time.

Footsteps rattle the ladder. Elliot pokes his head over the gutter. "Can I come up?"

I walk gingerly down the roof—loose grit from asphalt shingles can roll like little marbles—take Elliot's hand, and help him ease over from the ladder to the roof.

"What are you doing?" he asks.

"Well, I'm going to cut open the roof."

His eyes widen, ears perk. Knowing his father to be an incorrigible leg-puller, he's on the alert.

"No, what are you *really* doing?"

"I'm afraid I'm telling the truth. I'm going to cut the roof open up here at the ridge and build a little *raised* roof over the peak and install these ventilation strips." I show him the eight-foot-long-by-four-inch-wide strips of sheet aluminum, with louvers punched into the whole length.

"Why do you have to do that?"

"Well, when I built this roof sixteen years ago, I didn't include enough ventilation for the ceiling. If our house doesn't have enough fresh air flowing through the roof framing, then the moist air from our cooking and taking showers can get trapped in the house and condense in the ceiling. It could eventually saturate the insulation so much that water might start dripping down onto our sofa."

This is apparently more detail than Elliot is interested in, for he has plucked the chalk line from my tool belt, pulled a few feet of string out—blue chalk wafting on the breeze—and now he's reeling the line in, pretending he's fishing.

I don't really know whether I need this extra ventilation or not, but I've been haunted for some time by a story of a cabin that started drizzling *inside* because the ceiling wasn't vented. The owners came home from the store one day and found the place dripping like a cave. They had to completely remove the ceiling and replace their sopping insulation. They chuckled politely as they told me that story, because I was the one who had *built* that cabin. I had lived in it for a year in one of my more hermitic phases and I remember how snug it felt when I closed that lone door, the air pressure thumping at my eardrums. An admirably tight little box, I thought, but it was in fact a condensation trap.

When I heard that embarrassing story many years ago, I had resolved to immediately retrofit my own house with better ventilation. But then Elliot was born, and I got distracted and put off the roof job for seven more years.

I ease the big worm-drive saw down through the shingles and into the plywood. Elliot plugs his fingers in his ears as the saw blade sparks and howls. After a few minutes he waves good-bye, and climbs down the ladder. When I've sawed about halfway across the roof, I hit a nail. Suddenly the saw binds in the wood, kicks back faster than a horse, and now I'm sitting on my butt rubbing a bruised wrist, listening to the world thump like a heart. If I still smoked cigarettes, I'd roll one now.

Across the street, Mrs. Trindle comes out to scatter bread crumbs in her dusty driveway, and fill the birdbath—a garbage can lid on the ground—with fresh water. Mrs. Trindle must be seventysomething, skinny as a walking stick, and just as tough. She spends most days puttering in her yard, or racing around town in an old white Ford, running errands for shut-ins. She is the neighborhood's most reliable chicken-sitter: whenever any of the folks on the street who keep chickens need to be out of town, Mrs. Trindle will feed and water the flock and gather the eggs. I see her often, stalking down the street in a flower-print dress and barn boots, a red scarf over her gray hair and a basket on her arm, leaning into the morning with her brisk, stiff-legged gait. We all bring her fruits and vegetables from our gardens, and when Kapa sends Elliot over with a plate of cookies at Christmastime, she sends him back with one of those little store-bought pecan pies.

I watch Mrs. Trindle for a while puttering in her yard, trimming a rose bush with dull hand clippers, clamping onto a twig, then worrying the clippers back and forth. I hadn't noticed before that she's transplanted real pansies into her bed of plastic geraniums. A crow jumps down from the lilac bush into the bread crumbs and grabs the biggest chunk.

There's a line about crows in Hesiod's *Works and Days* that has always troubled me. Hesiod interrupts a run of outlandish farming advice to say, "When making a house, do not leave it unplaned, in case you get a raucous crow sitting on it and cawing." I'm not sure what "unplaned" refers to—shingles? clapboards?—but if rough construction can give you a case of crows, then our house might as well be plastered with them, or simply tarred and feathered. With its secondhand doors and windows, lumber salvaged from dismantled buildings, fixtures cannibalized from decrepit houses, sometimes snatched from the very jaws of bulldozers, Knot House is . . . well, rustic. Even most of the new lumber in the house is economy grade, riddled with knots and worm galleries.

I'm forever fixing things I should have done better the first time: replacing a leaky window, regrouting the tile around the kitchen sink. I learned each house-building skill as I went, my practice jobs often as not the final product. First-time visitors are often surprised to learn that Knot House is a new house. "Oh, I figured you'd remodeled it," they'll say. "It looks so . . . so *old*. I mean, like it's been here a while."

Maybe it's just a cover for my exaggerated frugality, but I *like* the look and feel and smell of old, gnarly stuff, things used, transformed once or twice so they've started to get the hang of metamorphosis. I'm probably just a low-down aesthete, a shabby-happy secondhand elitist. But why buy top-grade materials when I'll probably botch the installation anyway? I'm a poor carpenter after all, so I try to match the quality of the materials I buy to the quality of my workmanship, finding pleasure in an aesthetic of ineptitude.

Hesiod is right, though: shabby construction ruffles feathers. Kapa and I have a long-standing disagreement about the living room floor. It's made of hemlock, the softest of woods, two-by-six planks with gaps between them. The floor has a nineteenth-century farmhouse look to it, I like to think, though hemlock was simply all I thought I could afford when I started building. Finished with five coats of polyurethane, the wood has a nice gloss, but it's pocked with dents from chair feet, and gouged from gravel stuck in lug-soled boots, and Kapa has longed wished to lay an oak floor over the hemlock.

"Oak is expensive," I grumble, "and I don't know if my knees could handle laying a new floor." Two reasonable objections, but the truth is I just don't feature myself walking barefoot over a new oak floor. Too smooth, too hard, too uniform. No place for the imagination to get a purchase.

Kapa is patient, and even agrees with me in principle. She dresses herself elegantly in secondhand clothes. She considers our car, Henrietta, and our truck, Sparrowhawk—each nearly twenty years old—as part of the family. But she knows that secondhand has a hidden price, that sacrificing first quality aesthetically often means accepting second-rate usability, too, and maybe poorer longevity, or higher maintenance. She knows that the cracks between those poorly planed floorboards are full of dust, hair, noodles, carpet mites, and who knows what, and it gives her the heebie-jeebies. She sees the round pockmarks in the floor and worries they'll go to splinters. She wonders if we'll have the energy, or the money, to fix all our house problems when we're old.

By midmorning, I've cut the roof section away. As I peel the plywood off, I imagine myself flensing a whale, hacking away slabs of blubber, a butchery that whalers sometimes perform while the whale is still alive. Sheathing removed, I inspect the insulation: it's bone dry. I don't know whether to be disappointed that my work is for naught, or glad that no harm has been done. I toss the nailed-studded strips of plywood down into the front yard and take a breather. Across the street vireos and chickadees are flocking to Mrs. Trindle's bread crumbs. Two big scrub jays swoop into the lilac and raise a ruckus, scattering the smaller birds. Next comes a gray squirrel, and finally, flying in low and straight as a trident of guided missiles, three crows zoom in and fall on the crumbs.

It's been a couple of years since I've been inside Mrs. Trindle's house. Her senile husband was still alive then. The neighbors had warned me about Mr. Trindle's delusions of being a state trooper, told me how he would knock on their doors in the middle of the night and yell, "Don't worry! I'm here with my gun!" They still winced as they described the look of wounded betrayal on his face when the real police came, handcuffed him gently, and drove him to the hospital.

Mr. Trindle was housebound by the time I moved onto the street. When I'd visit them, he'd smile and wave from his overstuffed chair in the corner. He refused to wear a hearing aid, so a conversation with him was just like blowing bubbles. His mouth moved broadly, but his voice came out barely above a whisper.

"Hey, young fella."

"Morning, Mr. Trindle. How are you?"

"I used to be a policeman, you know."

"Yeah, I know that. Been getting out much?"

"Oh, I'm just tired of eating saltines."

One time when they were going to visit her family for a weekend, Mrs. Trindle asked me to feed their old spaniel, Perky. She showed me where to find the dog food and the leash, with never a hint of embarrassment for the shambles her house was in. I remember the murky-colored afghans covering the furniture, the piles of crumbly magazines in all the corners, the acrid smells. The house itself was decrepit, the floors canting this way and that so that neither the front nor the back doors would shut tightly enough to lock. The living room window was a mosaic of glass shards held in place by oodles of Scotch Tape, and the venetian blinds were as yellow as Mr. Trindle's teeth. Perky lifted his head once from his box in the corner, then flopped back flat. Mr. Trindle spoke quietly to the ceiling.

Perky died soon after that, and then, last year, Mr. Trindle died, too.

A couple of weeks ago, a flock of high school kids from Mrs. Trindle's church descended on her yard. They cleaned the gutters, raked leaves, pulled weeds. Two of the guys went up onto the roof with a caulking gun and slathered blackjack around the chimney flashing. They hammered a few more laths over the blue tarpaulin covering her roof. Then, as suddenly as

they'd come, the teenagers piled into their vehicles and drove
away. When I went out to the mailbox, Mrs. Trindle was sitting in her yard at the edge of the drainage ditch, weeding her
sweet peas.

"They sure got a lot done!" I called across the street.

"Some," she said. She looked pooped.

"Is there anything important that they didn't get to?"

She yanked at a dandelion. "Roof's bad. Always has been."

I looked at her tarp-covered roof, and muttered, "Yeah, that
will be a big job," and turned to studying my junk mail.

Late afternoon, now, dark clouds pooching over the Coast
Range. It might rain soon. I've got my little cupola framed up,
nailed the louvers into place, and sheathed the new raised
roof. Better tack some felt over the sheathing, and get my ass
off of here. I'll shingle the roof tomorrow.

Just for the hell of it—because I'm happy I'm almost done,
and scared of getting old, and ashamed that I don't do more to
help my neighbors—I let fly with a loud, gargly squawk:
KAW-KAW-KAW. The crows across the street look about nervously, abandon the bread crumbs, and fly up onto Mrs.
Trindle's roof, their glossy plumage black as stone blades
against the sky-blue of the tarp. Their claws poking holes in
the plastic, they gabble and dance there like three capricious
weather vanes.

Winter Garden

My gardening chores at the courthouse are few in the winter, but twice a week I drive downtown to pick up litter, rake leaves, deadhead the last of the season's roses. When my friend Andrew died in April, I sprinkled some of his ashes here under the rosebushes, and they're still visible, like flakes of fertilizer. Throughout the summer and autumn, I have postponed mourning his death—the grief inside me feels like a lump of unrisen dough. Now I sense a bout of memory coming on, but I resist it. There are clouds dark as asphalt lowering in the west, more rain is on the way, and I need to finish my chores while the weather holds.

The ground is so spongy from the autumn rains that I can no longer mow the lawns without leaving deep, muddy ruts. I load the riding mower onto its trailer and haul it back to the Parks Department shop, drain the gas tank, and chisel the dead black grass from the reels. The shop is poorly lit, and the radio—Mississippi John Hurt playing a twangy blues—buzzes with a bad speaker. Cold crawls up my legs from the concrete floor. Gradually a cloud gathers behind my forehead and my blood goes sluggish.

Winter always does this to me. I'll be doing my job, acting sane enough, when all my neurotransmitters seem to go dim, my thinking drifts, my muscles get mushy. It's as if my mind requires an infusion of dreaming before it will carry on, and I try not to fight or resent it. Usually if I surrender to the torpor for even a few minutes, I'm restored. But this winter, missing Andrew, not even trying to fathom his death, the downward pull has been deeper and more frequent. With an effort now, I finish pumping grease into the mower's zirts, then go lay my head on the lunchroom table and plummet into a fitful sleep.

I wake with a jerk at the sound of the boss's truck splashing into the parking lot. By the time he comes into the shop, I'm already up and busy sharpening an ax on the bench grinder, making a hellish racket. He waves, and goes to his computer. No doubt he sees how flushed and puffy my cheeks are, no doubt he knows what I've been doing. We all know about it. He has his own places for hidden sleeping. But we don't talk about it. What the underworld does with us in the winter must not be mentioned—it's too embarrassing, and it's inefficient.

I grind the ax's second bit, then pull out a wheelbarrow and take down from the tool rack a half dozen spades, three hoes, a grub hook. Sparks fountain over the edge of the metal, pricking my wrist. My mind settles into this useful violence with relief, its gaze narrowed to a field of view only a hand-breadth in diameter, intent on the collision between the spinning carborundum and the hoe's vulnerable steel.

Saturday, at home. Steady rain on the roof, a tedious mossy percussion. Midday outdoors and it's dark as dusk, weak-tea light filtered through miles of deep mist. Lying on the floor of my study, I watch a cobweb in the corner of the ceiling lift and settle on some current of air I can't feel. Two ladybugs crawl up the inside of the window glass while on the outside larvae of rain creep down. Close observation is an anchor against lethargy, but the floodwaters are rising—I feel the lights in my brain going out one by one.

Andrew did not like the rain. He was a bike rider and a serious gardener with a passion for thrifty living. Since he wouldn't own a car, but couldn't abide biking in the rain all winter, he bailed out every autumn and flew to Arizona, or Mexico, or the Big Island. When one of his cheerful letters would arrive, it would make me feel even more sluggish, unproductive, misplaced, and morose.

Downstairs, Elliot squawks—a head bump, or a clash with his mother—and then I hear Kapa cooing to him. I would not want my wife or my son to catch me asleep here—I told them I had work to do at my desk—so I lumber unsteadily to my feet. Looking out the window I see the garden paths are canals, the water table has returned to the surface. Our neighbor's two Romney ewes stand under her dead cherry tree like saturated sponges. The only cheerful thing in sight is Emil, our foot-high ceramic guardian of the herb beds, his Swiss cheeks still rosy over a bushy mustache, up to his lederhosen in standing water. The liquid sky leans heavily upon him, but Emil is unperturbed.

Now Elliot's racket has ceased. I suppose he and Kapa have gone downtown to the library as planned. But, no, here they are, asleep on the sofa, huddled together under the orange and brown afghan, the cat curled up at their feet. I creep back upstairs and lie down again. Lassitude, an intravenous solution, drips. I see Andrew smiling sadly at me as I fall back into something like sleep.

Monday afternoon, I'm holed up in the boiler room of the courthouse, waiting for a storm to pass. There's a workbench down here, and a desk where I sit reading Coyote stories: "Coyote and His Anus," "Coyote Takes Himself Apart," "Coyote Visits the Land of the Dead." Outside the street-level window, cars stroke past in a haggard rain. The furnace bellows steadily. Steam pipes knock and hiss. The sump pump in the floor drain kicks on like an idiot drummer, and I doze in my chair to the basement's strange music . . .

"Hello, Charles!" A woman's voice. One of the circuit court employees—what's her name? Before I can answer, she's grabbed her lunch out of the refrigerator and gone. I scan the room for something to fix on, something to hold me awake. On both sides of the door the walls are covered with circuit boards for the courthouse phone system, hundreds, thousands of little green, yellow, and red wires, insanely neat. Sometimes, down here in the winter, I imagine myself ripping out all those wires with a claw hammer.

Late morning, at home. Heavy gray clouds loom at the windows, a faceless presence. Geese honk somewhere over the house, lost in the mist. The rain, the lack of light, the loss of my friend, each tugs at me with a separate tentacle. Here's a photo Andrew sent me once from Cozumel: an empty beach, a tree-rimmed lagoon. His shadow on the sand directs the eye toward a little boat in the distance, upside down in the sand beside a smoldering campfire, from which a whisper of smoke rises.

I take up the baby food jar full of his ashes and turn it slowly in my hands. His three grown daughters and I each took a quarter of the ashes, a couple of pounds apiece in Ziploc bags. This is all that's left. I scattered handfuls under the blueberries at his old house, some here in our orchard, some in the river, a smidgen under a chair cushion in the public library. I didn't intend to save any, but I keep finding places where a bit of his chemistry should remain, and I don't want to run out now, so I'm down to disseminating tiny pinches here and there.

Some of his ash flakes are the size of rolled oats—bone chips, I suppose. In texture the ashes resemble a mix of cereal grains, like muesli. I wet my finger, touch it to the ashes—a few small grains stick. They taste slightly salty, then acerbic and very bitter. A sudden retch reflex. Saliva pumps quickly into my mouth, my throat swallows, eyes tear. When my heart quits racing and my fingers unclench, I feel drained, exhausted, but somehow clear, as if a fever had roared through me and, though still weak, I am on the mend.

I'm recalling a miserable winter's day when I worked as the supervisor of the county's corrections work crew. There are twelve of us, eleven petty criminals and me, grubbing out brambles and willows from a drainage ditch. We're sheathed in rain gear—yellow bibs and yellow slickers, barn boots and floppy black sou'westers—but the heavy drizzle still creeps down our necks. Muddy gloves slip on the shovel handles, ruining our grip. Water a foot deep runs in the trench; we keep losing our footing and plunging in.

I signal lunch. We pack ourselves into the sheriff's van and tear open our brown paper bags. The sandwiches are soggy, the coffee tepid. There is none of the usual joking and bragging, everyone quiet, sullen. The windows steam up. Rain hammers on the roof. In the seat beside me, a guy named Doug—wet black hair snaking down his cheeks—pulls out a knife and carefully pares his nails.

To be outdoors in winter, digging, weeding, tidying up the garden is a solace and a trial. Sometimes it's better to stay indoors and dream. Today I'm paging through one of my favorite books, *Winter Gardening in the Maritime Northwest*, a small, practical text, quietly encouraging, with little of the bombast of glitzier garden books. In fact, it is suffused with a deep and proper sadness: that the winter is long, that one must work, that disappointments are many and the act of cultivating one's own garden can only multiply them, but that one must do so anyway.

On page 49, there is a cogent discussion of cabbage maggots, with a very succinct and useful, "Cabbage Root Fly Egg-laying Chart." Further on, page 64, some timely advice about clubroot: "This slime mold is very persistent. . . . Don't give away plants that have soil from your garden attached to them: clubroot is no gift!"

Between showers, I wander out to the garden. Kapa planted two beds with brassicas back in the fall, mulched them heavily with aromatic mint compost, and here they sit, unconscious, awaiting spring. I fetch a bucket of ashes from the woodshed and sprinkle a thick ring around each plant. Kale, cabbage, purple sprouting broccoli, all need potash and an alkaline soil, but the main use for these ashes is to ward off the slugs. I spot three small slugs climbing a broccoli plant, pick them off, and hurl them over the fence.

Deep fog before dawn. Struggling awake in the gloom, I look out an upstairs window at the neighbor's sodium vapor lamp across the street, shrouded in drifting mist, wavering as if underwater. My brain, too, is foggy, my body sluggish. I know from experience that this torpid start on the morning will color my whole day, like a film of oil on water. Random encounters will appear suddenly double-exposed, a friend's face and his shadow face overlapping fuzzily. Conversations will blur with a bad echo, but I won't let on. I won't slur or tic. I will appear normal, and say nothing to anyone of this slight derangement, because, if communicating even our gross emotional weather makes us all uncomfortable, spelling out the subtleties of winter melancholia is hopeless.

It seems to me that the morning's psychic turbidity comes from the fog, *is* fog. The land engenders a range of moods, resonates with certain species of energy, and no one is exempt. Here, in the sodden Northwest, the place where the most massive forests on earth once grew, where the fish once thronged every river and rivulet, and the winter storms ruled the land half of each year as difficult but steadfast gods, the native emotions are still a winter-long melancholy and an opposing season of slavering gratitude.

Last winter, after the CAT scan revealed his brain tumor, Andrew stayed active. He experienced bouts of memory loss, headaches, and a gradual numbing of his left arm and leg, but well into April he was able to take care of himself, was still rid-ing his bike around town to say good-byes to old friends. Then, early on the morning of April 22, Earth Day, a few weeks shy of his sixty-ninth birthday, Andrew suffered a stroke. His daughter called and I went to sit with him. He was not conscious, his breathing was shallow and already his legs were starting to cramp and quiver from oxygen deprivation. His daughters and two other women, friends and caregivers, were there. We took turns holding him, massaging him, cooing and humming and talking him home.

My son's first grade class had a field trip to Finley Wildlife Refuge planned for that afternoon, and I had volunteered to go along and introduce the children to some plants and bugs. As the morning wore on and Andrew's powerful body labored on—in the absence, it seemed, of his spirit—I struggled with torn allegiances: should I stay with a dying friend to his last breath, or should I lead a troop of six-year-olds into the for-est? I knew that some of the children had never been on a hike in the woods before, that I could add centipedes and fawn lilies to their growing sense of world-and-self, but I knew also that I would never have a second chance to see my friend over the last threshold. His legs were trembling like a shook doll's now, his breathing gaspy and rattling. It was eas-ier for me to give him a last kiss, hug all the women there, and leave, and that's what I did. I've always been better at begin-nings than at endings.

The fog is thickening into rain now, as when confusion clarifies into pain. I rummage my bookshelves for a half-remembered creation myth: somebody makes a first human from ashes and rain. Coyote, maybe. The old world has been destroyed by fire, and Coyote comes along, jumping and twisting every so often, pretending he's a wind.

"I wish I had a friend," Coyote says. And he pats together some of the ashes, but they won't stick. He jumps and twists some more, but it doesn't start raining.

"I know," Coyote says, "I'll use some piss." And he pisses on the ashes and presses the gray mud into a shape.

And that's us.

Erratics

Elliot is fascinated with natural disasters lately. He's been checking out library books about volcanoes, earthquakes, hurricanes, tsunamis. He devours these stories of catastrophe as if he is trying to gauge the world's extremes, trying to get a handle on just how wild his life may get. Maybe it's a kind of immunilogical impulse: as we inoculate our bodies with small doses of disease to build up resistance, he is inoculating his psyche through manageable contacts with calamity.

Right now he and Kapa are on the sofa, looking at an album of photos we took when the Willamette River flooded in March 1996, when he was not quite three. Elliot points to a picture and says, "Look, there's Papa riding his bike through the water!" I remember how excited I was the whole time the river was out of its banks, how insanely I hoped it would keep rising higher and higher. That first morning of the flood, Kapa and I were washing the breakfast dishes, watching the rain pound down outside, when a car pulled into our driveway. A woman shrouded in a dripping, deep-hooded rain parka dashed onto our porch and knocked loudly. The second I opened the door the woman said, "I heard you might get flooded! You should come with me right now and stay at my house!" and I knew by her German accent it was Gertrude. I urged her inside.

Kapa said, "How kind of you to think of us!"

"But you are so close to the river!"

"Oh, I don't think our neighborhood will flood, Gertrude," I said. "We're pretty high above the river. But come and have a cup of tea."

"Oh, no! I must get home. I really think you should come, too. Don't bring anything. I have food, beds . . ."

"We're perfectly safe here, Gertrude," Kapa said, with a slight quiver of anxiety. "But thank you so much. If there is any problem later, we'll come stay with you." We hugged our friend, and she gave us a last mournful look and dashed back through the rain to her car.

In the previous three days, the valley had been deluged with fourteen inches of rain, and at the same time unseasonably warm air had melted much of the snowpack in the Cascades. The valley soils, saturated for weeks, could absorb no more. Kapa and I had talked on the phone to neighbors earlier in the morning, so we already knew that the Mill Race had over-flowed its banks and flooded both our street, Crystal Lake Drive, and two of the four lanes of South Third Street, the lone thoroughfare that connects south Corvallis with downtown.

We knew there were flood warnings in effect for the Willamette River and many of its tributaries, and Crystal Lake Drive *was* the street closest to the river. But Gertrude's visit was the first we'd heard about the possibility of our immediate neighborhood flooding. Our neighborhood is up on a bench, with a quarter mile of low-lying park and farmland between ourselves and the river. We were on high ground—we thought.

Gertrude's visit had left us feeling uneasy, so we decided to go survey the situation ourselves. We tucked Elliot into the bike trailer and pedaled toward downtown. The rain had let up temporarily and the clouds had lifted a bit. Behind the fiberglass factory, the road to the boat ramp disappeared into open water. The Willamette was swollen to eight or ten times its normal width, inundating the cornfield on this side of the river and stretching way out across the gravel quarries, grass seed fields, and scrub forest lands on the far side. The floating dock at the boat ramp had risen to the very top of its pilings. If the river rose a foot higher, the dock would float free and go sailing toward Portland.

Where Crystal Lake Drive dipped down to cross the Mill Race, we came upon a hundred yards of open water. To find our everyday street transformed into water was both exciting and disturbing. And something else: I noticed how the silt-colored water revealed the topography of the land. I had not known that that gentle rise beyond the bridge matched this nearer slope so gracefully. Something about the sight reminded me of how I loved to gaze at the top of Elliot's head when he was an infant, studying the topography of his skull, marveling at how the bones fit together under his scalp. When I looked up, clouds were roiling massively from the southwest.

We backtracked to Alexander Avenue and biked out to Third Street to find the entire road inundated, changed into a lake a half-mile long. Sheriff's deputies had set up a roadblock by Lincoln Elementary School to turn away nonessential traffic. A dump truck plowed slowly toward us through the flood, sending waves lapping against the glass wall of the Honda motorcycle showroom. People were everywhere, gawking and trading gossip. In the shopping center parking lot, boys were playing soccer on Rollerblades, using a rust-eaten Toyota pickup for the goal. At the wheel of the truck, a long-haired man sat drinking coffee, heedless of the occasional *wump* on the passenger side door. Whenever the soccer ball rolled into the water, one of the boys would skate headlong into the flood, sending up a shower of spray.

Elliot heard a backup beeper—his favorite sound on earth—and spotted the dump truck again, backing around the school building. The moment it began spilling its load of sand, a dozen people with shovels and empty gunnysacks attacked the new pile and soon began chucking full sandbags into the back end of a station wagon. Another dump truck entered the water from the north, and a bright yellow kayak darted from the parking lot of the Orchard Motel to surf in the truck's wake. A fly fisherman cast his line toward a half-submerged dumpster. From a flooded side street, a man and a woman waded beside a canoe in which an old black Labrador, pink tongue lolling, sat like a god. I wandered over to see what a bevy of photographers at the curb had discovered, and found a manhole cover in the street gushing foot-high jets of water, six pretty fountains. Enjoying the air of festivity, I had not no-

ticed another air: sewage. But I didn't mention it to Kapa because I had decided to enter the flood.

When I told her I wanted to ride my bike downtown
through the water, Kapa rolled her eyes at me, and said,
"That's really risky!"

"Maybe a little," I said. "But I promise I'll be home in an
hour."

I kissed her and Elliot good-bye, and cycled into the flood.
In the shallows, the pedaling was easy, and I was driving re-
sponsibly in the right-hand lane. But when the pedals began
going under water, there was a sideways force I had to com-
pensate for. The floodwaters had appeared to be a placid lake,
but now I felt the truth: this was a river in spate. Water was
over the crank, and I had to give the pedals everything I had.
A sheriff's truck entered the water at the far end, heading my
way. I moved farther to the right, and suddenly the water
deepened almost over my wheels. The thrust of the current
was on my thighs now, pushing me sideways. Then my wheel
grazed the curb and I almost fell, but I got a foot out onto the
sidewalk just in time and stopped and braced myself, water
swirling about my waist. As the sheriff's deputy drove by, he
glanced over, then looked deliberately away from me, another
damn fool water-biker beneath his notice.

When I finally emerged from the flood and hit dry pave-
ment again, I felt clean and light as a baby duck. I waved to the
deputies manning this end of the roadblock, and pedaled up
onto the high bridge over the Willamette. The bridge was
closed, deserted, and all mine. A high bridge empty of all traffic is an exhilarating place. With the river surging below,

cleaving around the pilings, the bridge thrummed as if powered by huge diesel engines deep in its bowels.

I urged the flood higher. I wanted to see the river rake houses off foundations, drown used-car lots, bury golf courses under silt, shake bridges to slabs, take back the whole drained-and-filled valley.

I weasel in between Kapa and Elliot on the sofa. They're looking at a photo of a school bus driving down Third Street, through water almost up to the bright yellow sides. "What do you remember about the flood, Elliot?"

"I remember riding on this school bus. They used it instead of the city bus, didn't they? Because it had higher wheels? And when we walked around downtown, the stores had sandbags in front of their doors. And a big chunk of riverbank fell into the water, didn't it?"

"Yeah, just north of the highway bridge. Did I ever tell you about some *really* big floods, the Missoula Floods? No? Well, this happened maybe about twelve thousand years ago, near the end of the last ice age. There was this enormous lake, Lake Missoula, high up in the Rocky Mountains, and what kept the waters of this lake penned up there in the mountains was *ice,* deep walls of ice that dammed up the passes through the mountains. But the climate all around the world just then was warming up; the vast sheets of ice that covered Canada were melting back around the edges, and what happened is—the ice dams that held back Lake Missoula started to get soft and get some cracks in them, and then, *whammo,* they broke.

"Now, I'm not talking about a *leak* in the dam. I'm talking about a complete collapse. Millions and billions of gallons of lake water, chock-full of icebergs, boulders, and debris roared out of the Rockies like a herd of bulldozers."

"But what happened to the people when the flood came?"

"That's a good question. I don't know if anybody lived around here way back then."

"But if there were people here, they probably climbed a hill. That's what I'd have done."

"Yeah, me, too, if I had enough time. . . . Anyway, you want to know how scientists figured out about the floods? Some really strange things that people had been noticing for a long time were these huge boulders that are plopped on top of ridges all around the Willamette Valley and up in Washington State, too. They are big as cars. Geologists called them *erratics,* which means wanderers, because when they analyzed the *kind* of rock the boulders were made of, the geologists could tell that those boulders did not come from around here. There are no rocks like these in the Cascades or the Coast Range. So it just seemed like they wandered here from somewhere else. Where did they come from? And how did they get there?"

"A volcano blasted them!"

"Good guess. But no, they're too big, and the wrong kind of rock."

"Well, how *did* they get here?"

"Remember that huge lake up in the Rockies . . ."

"Did the boulders come down when the ice dam broke?"

"Yeah, but . . . do boulders float?"

"No . . ."

"What if they were frozen in icebergs . . ."

"And the icebergs floated!"

"And then the flood drained away . . ."

"And the icebergs melted!"

"Erratic!"

Why do I feel such glee at the thought of a boulder-floating flood four hundred feet deep where my house now stands? Why do I get such a charge out of witnessing the power of nature? Does it work like slapstick comedy: I laugh because I'm *not* the one who stepped on the skateboard and went splat? I wasn't here when the Missoula Flood struck, ha-ha! So the prospect of a catastrophe in another place or another time makes me feel safe, and either smart or lucky?

But that doesn't explain why I wanted to bicycle right into the flood, or why it excited me so much to feel the highway bridge trembling at its roots. I am not what you'd call a thrill seeker. I have no interest in bungee jumping or hang gliding. But maybe natural disasters wake me up, remind me not to take my life for granted, not to forget that I could be forced at a moment's notice to abandon my comfortable routines. And there's this: haven't we all noticed how, in the wake of a disaster, there's a blossoming of cooperation and caring? People seem softened by catastrophe, more porous and interconnected, their best natures given free rein.

So how wild can the world get? No doubt wilder than any of us can imagine. Would I welcome another Missoula Flood, a mountain of water and ice hundreds of feet high hurtling faster than a train down the Columbia and up the Willamette Valley? Of course not. All I can really say is that to contemplate the forces of nature in the scale of geologic time feels humbling, and exhilarating. It stretches my imagination. If there is something like sinew that connects my heart and my brain, big floods tug at it, keep it flexible. As hard as my brain works to file experiences into categories, a natural disaster tosses the system to shambles.

I'm not knocking orderliness. I treasure the mind's innate synthesizing of experience into meaning. I just need reminders that the source of all those organizing categories is chaos, the unpredictable and ever-generative *wild*. And what a blessing it would be if I could learn to see my ordinary, everyday experiences that way! To feel my brain humming at the sight of a mason bee nectaring on a plum blossom, say. Or to sense the quivering of the infinite as I watch Elliot practice writing his cursive capital Q. Seven-year-olds seem to be in that zone of elevated curiosity a good deal of the time. It might be an attitude worth cultivating, come what may.

Homemade Windows

Early Saturday morning, looking out my study window. Winter and spring are having a tussle outside. In the neighbor's backyard a plum tree is in full blossom, like a gaudy, house-high pink hyacinth. Between that tree and our house, however, the air is full of blowing snow, thick flakes tumbling and sticking together, piggybacking themselves into strange aggregations, like brief, elaborate junk sculptures. The snow and the blossoming tree are lovely, but this morning I'm most interested in the window itself. This is a window of my own making. It is not invisible, not even so simply transparent. A window is not supposed to have a history, but this one does.

"Windows are the wounds in a house." That's what my carpenter friend Elmer says. "It's a shame," he told me once, "how we take the skin of a house, a nice, impervious surface, and cut a bunch of holes in it. That's where all the trouble starts." He means that around the doors and windows is where leaks begin, where moisture, every building's arch-antagonist, seeps in. Then doors will warp, windows stick, sills rot.

I know what Elmer is talking about, because I have a bad case of rotting windows. One of the things I need to do today is plan the next round of replacements: the window with the S-curve crack above Kapa's easel, the window on the landing that has leaked rainwater into Elliot's cubbyhole under the stairs, the window above the kitchen sink whose leaky vacuum seal has let a permanent fog in between the two panes of glass. Although it is just mid-March, I must order new windows now if I want to get them delivered by mid-July.

New houses generally get factory-built windows, and they are among the most expensive parts of a house. But I built my own. I bought the glass first, thermopane blanks from a place in Deadwood that specializes in seconds. Then I built the frames. I cut two-by-eights to length and rabbeted one side so that when they were assembled into a rectangular frame there was a recessed pocket all around to set the panes into. I laid a strip of glazier's tape in each side of the rabbet, set the glass against the tape, nailed three-fourths-inch quarter-round stops on each side, and applied silicone caulking to keep the moisture out. It took me a long time to build the eighteen windows in the house, but I saved thousands of dollars.

However, they leaked. I didn't install flashing at the headers, or bevel my sills to channel the rain off. My windows were a slow disaster, and now a pain in the ass. We've been replacing them with store-bought, aluminum-clad, wooden windows with built-in weather flashing, a few at a time as we can afford them, the worst leakers first. The very worst windows were in the mud room, my most bogus installation, three big sheets of thermopane glass I set directly into the wall framing. Sloppy construction, they leaked from day one; we could see the dampness and water stains spreading on the sill. Putting one's faith in silicone caulking is an existential mistake. Elmer and I replaced those windows last summer. He had some fancy aluminum flashing with rubber gaskets that press tightly against the glass. "A permanent kiss," he called it. "Guaranteed not to leak."

Elmer believes there are doors and windows in the soul, as well, unfortunate as that may be, and you had better frame your walls square, and set your jambs plumb, and weatherstrip every crack, or your soul will leak out. Your moral compass will lose its fluid and dry up and you'll no longer be able to see your own way. Or else the world will get in and rot your soul from within. That's why there are no doors or windows in Eden, Elmer says, because paradise has no inside and outside. If there is a wall around that garden, there is nothing beyond the wall. Not even thought can go there. But put a window in the wall and now there are two worlds, and now there can be stories, the imagination can wander, and the leaking begins.

Elmer is not a prophet of good cheer but of solid, if gloomy, sensibility. In the Renaissance the individual soul was seen as something *made,* hammered and forged in the smithy of everyday life, and melancholy, a feeling for the irreducible sadness of things, was the only solid foundation to build on. Melancholy and all the subtle kinds of depression that we moderns are so poor at distinguishing, much less appreciating, are the cellars and basements where Saturn speaks his elder truths to wistful youth. The Jungian psychologist Thomas Moore says, "Dreams . . . often depict construction sites and buildings just going up, suggesting again that the soul is *made*: it is the product of work and inventive effort. . . . The 'children of Saturn' traditionally included carpenters, shown in drawings putting together the foundations and skeletons of new houses."

Elmer could be a foreman for Saturn Construction. Elmer can make a door stop squeaking with a stern word. He can drive nails with his eyes.

I remember a science article I read years ago about a cow in whose side scientists had cut a hole and installed a window. They wanted to see her several stomachs in action. Isn't that the basic technology of literature? Don't we hope to understand the guts of people as much as their souls, to see just how they grind it out? Think of Swede Levov, in Philip Roth's *American Pastoral*, after his daughter has blown up the town post office and killed a doctor. He's on the phone, listening to a stranger telling him where he can find his daughter, and he lifts the roof off a cardboard model of his new house: inside, all the rooms are furnished in intricate toy detail—a loveseat, the canopied bed, real-looking little books on the bookshelves—and he realizes his wife is leaving him for the architect. You can see the acids slosh in his stomach, see the ulcer growing on his duodenum.

Last week I went for a walk on a cloudy night without moon or stars, cold enough for a hat and gloves. I walked down the dark street to the corner, disappointed that all my neighbors had pulled their drapes. But coming back, I could see from a distance that *our* house was all lit up and none of the curtains drawn. I stood in the street hoping Kapa would appear at the study window, and she did! She walked by holding up a length of fabric, envisioning a sewing project. I thought of Ruth in Marilynne Robinson's *Housekeeping,* how she keeps imagining—with the house lit, the world outside dark—strangers looking in at her. Yet when she looks at the window, she sees only her own reflection.

I went into the backyard and looked in Elliot's window. He had gone to bed before I left, but his light was still on. He sleeps in a bed suspended from the ceiling, and I had to crouch down to be able to see up to where he lay, propped on one elbow, reading a picture book: *Young Lancelot.* He was in another country. What a tremendous distance I felt from him, my little boy, my eight-year-old knight. God, I missed him.

I knew that if he glanced out the window and saw a shadowy face gazing in, he would be frightened. Just the night before he had woken up scared. Wakeful myself, I heard him gasp, then clamber down the ladder from his bed and dash into our room. "I'm scared," he whimpered, and weaseled under the covers into his mother's arms. What did he hear? What did he dream? He would never tell us. Whatever scared him had gone back through some doorway into the dark where it must not be betrayed.

So seeing depends on being in the dark? You can't look from light into darkness? Wouldn't that make evil almost impossible to see, unless you went even farther into that darkness? I went inside. I locked the back door, though there's no dead bolt and any burglar could slip the latch in a second.

Sometimes after dark I turn off the lights and stand for a while at the mud room windows looking out at the stars, big, prickly burrs of light. The thermopane windows do that—the two sheets of glass blur the image, shatter and bangle the starlight. Then, if I take off my glasses the light-splatter gets even wilder, prettier, but dizzy, the burly swirls playing havoc on my inner ear.

Outside, the snow is melting as fast as it lands. Where flakes have crashed into the window, now there are distinct beads of water evenly spaced on the glass, each bead shaped like a tiny face looking in. Moisture fogs the interior space between the double panes of glass: the seal has failed. This window, too, needs replacing.

I hear the rattle of the copper-pipe railing around Elliot's bed. Good, he'll be up before the snow is all melted. Maybe we'll dash out and make a snowman. I type quickly, hoping to finish this before he comes upstairs to nuzzle into my lap. I have a new pair of bifocals, and neither of the two lenses focuses exactly on my computer screen. I keep shifting my head up and down, trying now this angle, now that, searching for clarity. If you looked in the window and saw me typing, you'd think I was being asked a question over and over, and repeatedly nodding yes.

Book House

Elliot brings home from school a little house made from a cardboard box, open on one side so you can see in. He's partitioned off four rooms, two upstairs and two down, by taping in walls and floors of cardboard, and added a bed, a refrigerator, a sofa, and a coffee table all made of cardboard (crudely, for Elliot, like his father, is not a meticulous craftsperson). The clever thing about the house, and the learning goal for the project, is that it's wired for electric lights: each room has its own small flashlight bulb poking through the ceiling. The wiring circuit is taped onto the back of the box: a power plant of four AA batteries, slender black and red wires snaking to all corners, and switches made out of paper clips pinned to the box so that they can swivel to open or close against contacts made of brass paper clasps.

His fourth-grade teacher likes doing hands-on projects like these, and the kids love them. Elliot can picture now how the light switches in our house work, breaking or completing the circuit at the hot bus bar within the switch, and he can imagine how the wiring loops around within our walls from switch to outlet to switch, all emanating from the breaker panel in the kitchen. He knows what the plastic insulation on the wires is for, why it works, and how to use a wire stripper to peel the insulation away from the copper wire inside.

I did all the wiring for our house, set up the breaker box, installed the switches and outlets, and strung all the wires. I got an electrician to teach me the basics, and then I followed the instructions in a book. People often stare at me pop-eyed, a little shocked, when I mention that I wired my own house. Like, "What kind of moron are you? Any dope knows you don't mess with electricity!" But wiring is idiotically simple. All the terminals are clearly marked + or −. There is absolutely no ambiguity about it, just positive and negative. And, secret of secrets: when you're wiring a new house, there is no electricity in the wires! It isn't hooked up yet. There is no risk whatsoever until you connect to outside power at the meter, and the Uniform Building Code requires that homeowners leave that one final task to a licensed electrician.

For working around live circuits, a professional electrician is worth union scale. But stringing wires in new construction is mostly just grunt work, and I knew I could save a lot of money doing it myself. So, after I had the shell of my house dried-in, I called some electric contractors. I explained that

I wanted to do my own wiring, but I was looking for a professional I could pay to walk me through the process of wiring new
construction, show me some of the tricks, answer my questions
if I got stuck along the way and, finally, come and hook up the
meter to live service when I'd completed my part of the job. All
the electricians in the phone book chuckled me off. The one
reply I remember—"I'm an electrician, not a nanny!"—was
typical of the lot. But then a carpenter friend told me of an electrician who worked part-time out of his house who might be
willing to take me on. He gave me a phone number.

Jerry was a jumpy little guy, incredibly high strung, a
part-time Pentecostal minister. The thought of him working
around live circuits was scary, for he talked nonstop and
never had his mind wholly on what he was doing. He quoted
scripture while showing me how to strip insulation and
crimp wires. But I was paying him by the hour, and I really
didn't want the meter running while he practiced homilies
on me. Normally a glutton for metaphor, I wanted from Jerry
nothing but shop talk, so I ignored his sermonizing and heard
only the electrical lore. If I had it to do over, I might try to
hear both.

After Jerry got me started, I bought a book, a pair of wire
strippers, all the necessary supplies, and I plunged in, nailing
up outlet boxes, drilling holes in the studs, pulling 14–2
sheathed cable to all the rooms. My trusty copy of *Basic Home
Wiring Illustrated* was always close at hand, like an exception-
ally calm and tolerant father, perfectly clear and never conde-
scending, a mentor of the highest order. My flesh-and-blood
father was a wonderful man, but a certified klutz, and unin-
terested in things mechanical. I got my desire to build a house

not from him, but from books, and books have been some of my best teachers in every stage of house building.

These days many of us must look to the written word for all kinds of instruction, guidance, and inspiration that once came more directly from family and community members. The poet (and house builder) Gary Snyder describes the gift of books this way: "My grandparents didn't tell stories around the campfire before we went to sleep—their house had an oil furnace instead, and a small collection of books. I got into their little library to entertain myself. In this huge old occidental culture, our teaching elders are books. For many of us, books are our grandparents."

Why is it that these days so little of our cultural wisdom is handed down through intimate, intergenerational teamwork? Isn't it sad that girls and boys don't work side by side with their mothers, fathers, aunts, and uncles very much anymore? Still, I am grateful for my books. Books instructed me in many of the skills I needed, and even more important, books inspired me to want to build a house in the first place, books like Henry David Thoreau's *Walden*, Henry Beston's *The Outermost House*, Wendell Berry's *The Long-legged House*.

If books ignited in me the idea of building a house, they influenced me in a very different and heavier way, too. I first moved to Oregon in the autumn of 1974, hitchhiking across the country with just fifty dollars in my pocket and a backpack full of camping gear. When I think of the stuff I've acquired in the intervening years, that youthful portability looks pretty romantic. But as quick as I had settled into a cheap Portland apartment and found a job, I called my mother back in Ohio and asked her to ship me several big boxfuls of books. Among them were several books about houses, including Bernard Rudofsky's wonderful *Architecture without Architects,* full of photos of yurts and thatched huts, cave dwellings, and houses carved out of the trunks of live baobabs; S*helter,* a big compendium of building ideas edited by Lloyd Kahn; *The Whole Earth Catalog;* and back issues of *Mother Earth News.* By the time I was thirty, I'd bought and lugged from apartment to apartment so many books, boxes and boxes of books, that their sheer weight was gradually wearing down my mobility, making me long for a home. Home, I thought then, would be the place where you build permanent shelves for your books.

And then there were the weightless books that wanted a home as well: the books I hoped to write. Having experienced the power of books to change the course of my life, to inspire me to previously unknown ambitions, I understood literature as a gift that had to be passed on. And I felt most alive when I was writing.

I think the wiring in my house would have come out all right without Jerry's help, though it would have taken me a lot longer. But I couldn't have done it without a good manual like *Basic Home Wiring Illustrated.* It's a formula I followed time and again in building the house: some hands-on experience and a reliable how-to book. I'm glad Elliot is getting to wire a toy house in fourth grade, because school is usually *too* bookish, all those facts left dangling in the air, unhoused.

What if, in high school, students could choose home building as the focus for all their studies: how to build a real house on an actual lot in their own town, and how to be good citizens and neighbors. Every subject would be covered to the usual standards—reading, writing, mathematics, history and civics, all the sciences—and everything studied in the context of

Home. John Dewey described the idea in a letter to his wife, Alice. "There is an image of a school growing up in my mind," he wrote, "a school where some actual & literal constructive activity shall be the centre & source of the whole thing. . . . I can see, theoretically, how the carpentry etc. involved in building a model house should be the centre of a social training."

Every place would do it a little differently, of course. Every region would want to consult its own lore and literature for stories about what does and doesn't work. Here's a rough outline for a possible curriculum for the Willamette Valley.

Grade 9

English: literature of the Willamette Valley: *Moontrap,* Don Berry; *Coyote Was Going There,* Barry Lopez; *Always Coming Home,* Ursula LeGuin

Writing: poetry and prose writing on home, neighbors, local critters, and plants

Carpentry I: bookshelves and birdhouses

Mathematics: geometry and algebra applied in measuring and cutting; balancing a checkbook

Chemistry and Home Economics: cooking and baking; cleaning products, how they work and how they degrade; water and sewage treatment

Ecology: chaotic structure of a sunflower; galaxy formation

Grade 10

English: literature of the American West: *Huckleberry Finn,* Mark Twain; *Myths & Texts,* Gary Snyder; *Housekeeping,* Marilynne Robinson

Writing: the art of complaining: letters to the editor; oral histories; family histories

Carpentry II: garden construction: arbors, trellises, benches

History: history and prehistory of the Pacific Northwest; *Ishi*, Theodora Kroeber

Applied Chemistry, Physics, and Mathematics: welding, soldering, painting, plumbing; ecological impacts of industrial chemicals

Art: drawing, painting, and drafting your dream house

Grade 11

English: world literature: *Walden,* Henry David Thoreau; *Howard's End,* E. M. Forster; *One Hundred Years of Solitude,* Gabriel García Márquez; *The Issa Valley,* Czeslaw Milosz; "The Bear," William Faulkner

Carpentry III: beginning cabinetry

Applied Geography, Civics, and Land Use Planning: apply for building permit; attend Land Use Planning Board meeting

Art: constructing scale models of houses and civic buildings

Grade 12

English, Writing, Civics, Ecology, Art: conversing with the community: reading, writing, and speaking out on local issues in education, ecology, landscape, and architectural design; keeping a lifetime illustrated journal

Carpentry IV: apprenticeship with Habitat for Humanity

And what if, upon successful completion of this high school program, each student received vouchers from the state or federal government—that is, from all of us, acting collectively through our democratic institutions—for either (1) the cost of a college education at a state university, or (2) the same amount of money to be applied toward the purchase of land, materials, and labor costs for building a little starter house?

Of course, most of us think teenagers just out of high school don't want to start a home and settle down, don't want to be adult members of a vital community. We suppose they're not interested in securing some real economic assets and a genuine emotional investment in a neighborhood. But maybe that's only because in twelve years of schooling, it's a possibility nobody ever mentioned!

I'm recalling a rainy night last winter when I was reading a book aloud to Elliot and Kapa, the two of them stretched out on the sofa, heads at either end, legs interlaced. The plush noise of rain on the roof enclosed us in a nest of sound. The woodstove added a little whistling, and the lamp on the end table flickered occasionally. I was reading *The Wheel on the School* by Meindert DeJong, a wonderful story about some kids at a little village school who scour the Dutch countryside for an old wagon wheel to mount on their school roof to entice storks to nest there. The children undergo some remarkable trials and change their entire community in the process. One of the children was trying to salvage a wheel from an old abandoned boat mired deep in mud. The tide had just come in and stranded the child on the boat, when suddenly a big gust of wind rocked our house and the power went out. Kapa groaned, but Elliot hopped up, rummaged in the dark for stick matches and lit a candle.

As the wind continued buffeting the house, and I leaned close to the candle, searching for the place on the page where I'd left off, Elliot, lying with his hands behind his neck, gazing up at the ceiling where candle shadows danced, sighed loudly and said, "Nothing like a good book on a stormy night."

Remodeling the Hovel

I dig another nail head out of the old siding with the cat's-paw, slip a crowbar around it, and draw the 16d sinker out. The squawk of the nail letting go jangles my nerves. If an unwelcome memory wanted to announce itself with a noise, the cry of a rusty nail would do the job.

"Elliot, hand me my hammer."

He fetches the tool, then sits in the corner jingling a coffee can full of bent nails.

What we're doing is detaching the eight-foot-square lean-to room I once cobbled onto the side of the shop. We're planning to jack it up, slide some skids under it and tow the room with the pickup to its new home next to Elliot's swing set. After I add a miniature deck and a mattress-sized loft, it will become Elliot's playhouse, a present for his sixth birthday. Kapa plans to sew him some curtains and help Elliot paint a mural on the walls. But first, all the hardware that holds the room to its past use has to be removed, without gouging the wood any more than necessary.

Elliot asks, "Can I pull a nail?"

"Sure. Let's try this smaller nail. Here, take the cat's-paw . . ."

"Why is it called a cat's-paw?"

"Well, see how the end curls under like a cat's paw? And it claws out nails."

"I get it."

"Hold it at an angle—like this—against the wood, so the sharp edge of the paw will dig in under the nail head, then tap the back of the paw with your hammer. Here, try it."

There's a knack to it, of course, managing two tools with the proper tension. Once, twice, the cat's-paw slides off, but on the third try Elliot gets the edge started right and the tool buries itself neatly in the wood and curls under the head. He levers out the nail.

"I did it!" he says, inspecting his trophy. "Can I keep this nail?"

"What for?"

He shrugs. "Just to show I could do it."

A week later, early May, and the apple trees are blooming in the orchard. Instead of the fragrance of flowers, though, there's a burned-rubber odor in the air, from the pickup's toasted clutch. Towing the clubhouse—Elliot insists we call it clubhouse, rather than playhouse—was almost more than the Toyota could handle. The wheels spun, the clutch slipped, Elliot and Kapa yelled encouragement, and finally, grudgingly, the old room moved. Now it sits beside its new foundation, a hexagram of four-by-six floor joists on concrete peer blocks, awaiting the next step.

Some of our friends are supposed to stop by at two o'clock and help us lift the clubhouse onto its new foundation. I've bolted a pair of handles—twelve-foot-long two-by-fours, one on each side of the room—for us all to grab onto. Right on time Russell shows up, then Joan, Gregg, Joe, Sharon, and Larry, several of them with a child or two in tow.

This job could take five minutes, or it may not work at all—the room may be just too heavy. We line up along the handles like pallbearers beside a coffin, I count three, and we hoist the clumsy old room straight up, shuffle forward, slide it onto the new floor joists, and, voilà, a clubhouse. The kids cheer, then jostle inside, stomping on the floor, screaming together at the top of their lungs as if performing some kind of shock-cleaning, scouring ghosts out of the corners.

Now it's a month later, mid-June, and Elliot has shown little interest in his clubhouse. School's out and he's home all day, but he rarely plays there. Occasionally he and his playmates will crayon elaborate membership cards at the kitchen table, vote for officers, and all run to the clubhouse. But, a few minutes later, they're back outside again, climbing the willow, or kicking the soccer ball, or they've flipped the canoe upright in the grass and are paddling off on another fantasy. I think he likes having the clubhouse, but he doesn't use it. Maybe in another few years, when he needs a little more distance from Kapa and me.

I keep wanting things for Elliot that he doesn't want yet, may never want. Last year, for his fifth birthday, it was a swing set, the year before that, roller skates. This year, the clubhouse, with its nifty, kid-sized door, two windows that really open, even a little front porch. But I can see now that it just doesn't captivate him. The other day he said he wanted to put a shelf by the window. I praised his simple design, helped him select a board, saw it to length, attach a pair of brackets, and screw the brackets to the wall. It came out pretty well, but the only prize possession he's placed on it so far is the bent nail.

Meanwhile, I've begun to sort through the old memories still clinging to the room, and realized some of them are stories I need to pass on to Elliot. It may not be necessary to attach a story to a place. It may be that stories have plenty of body themselves. But if this particular story is housed in this club-house in our backyard, maybe it will be there someday if he really needs it.

Elliot's clubhouse was originally my writing shack. I knocked it together one weekend soon after Kapa moved into the house with me. I called it the Hovel, my getaway space, and for a few months I spent a couple of hours there every day. It was furnished with a card table, a straight-backed chair I bought from a convent, a little space heater, and an ashtray. I went there to write, to smoke and drink, to be alone.

These days I prefer to write in the very early morning, be-fore Kapa and Elliot are awake, with a cup of strong coffee coaxing me over the threshold between dream and thought. I like thresholds, in-between places, the moments when reality shifts and creaks, when veins of molten eternity gush into the sedimentary layers of time. I like solid prose that all of a sud-

den goes weird-flavored and musical, because in those morning hours at my desk, that's how life tastes and sounds.

But when I was still a bachelor, my favorite threshold was
early evening. I worked all day as a gardener, and all weekend
building my house, and after eight hours of manual labor had si-
phoned away my rationality, reduced me to a dumb animal—
abrutissement, the French call it—I'd get a half rack of beer and
a pack of cigarettes, and I'd write. The nicotine would constrict
my blood vessels, the sugars in the beer perk up my slack body,
the alcohol induce a dreamy fluidity, and I'd get a good hour or
two of happy scribbling before sagging into stale stupidity.

But when Kapa moved into the house with me, it cramped
my evening ritual. She couldn't abide the smoke, or the sight
of me turning every night from an alert human being into a
grinning effigy. So I built the Hovel, where I could carry on
my career unobserved, while alone in the house, having been
stiff-armed by my habit, Kapa fumed.

My father was such a sweet drunk. At neighborhood cocktail
parties, at holiday gatherings, or on long, lazy Saturday after-
noons, he swizzled old-fashioneds or gin and tonics, becoming
playful and giddy, then mushy and remote, then stumbling
and defensive, then slurrily contrite. There must have been
late-night confrontations when my mother tried to reason with
him, plead with him, shame him. I can imagine her, in desper-
ation, pummeling my father with all sorts of names—"Drunk-
ard! Coward! Selfish bastard!"—but I can only hear my father
whimper in submission. Did he try to appease her, or bully or
shame her? I can't imagine him striking her, can't even picture
him lambasting her with profanity, but I know that in the grip

of his drug he may have become unrecognizable to me. Before I was ten, my father was gone, moved away to California where his brother had found him a job.

There may have been some horrible scenes, and I may have overheard some of them, but I don't remember. I don't remember much at all from those years, far less it seems to me than my friends typically remember of their childhoods. I can picture the faces of my schoolmates, but can't recall many names. I have a poor long-term memory in general, aggravated, I suspect, by moving away from friends so often when I was a child. After my mother and father split up, my mother went to work managing cafeterias at small colleges in Ohio and Illinois, and she was good at it, so she got promoted and transferred to a new job every year. From third grade to high school graduation, I attended twelve different schools. I had to work at learning new names, not remembering old ones. I would never see those friends again anyway, and remembering them only made me feel miserable.

Elliot wants to know what the spirit level is for.

"The level shows us if our studs are standing vertical, or 'plumb,'" I explain.

"Are they?" he asks.

"Well, let's see. Hold it this way—plumb tube up—along this stud. See the two lines on the tube? Is the bubble exactly between the lines?"

"No."

"That's right. So this stud is out of plumb, it's not vertical, not straight up and down."

"Why isn't it plumb? Will it hurt anything?"

Oh, Elliot, you ask such good questions. When I nailed up this wall, I think I knew—hoped—that my drinking days were numbered. When Kapa moved into the house with me, I could feel a gathering of momentum toward family and domesticity, and though I was scared of it, scared of my bad habits being exposed, scared of losing my solitude, scared of being responsible for anyone but myself, I wanted a chance to be a husband and a father.

The Hovel was my last stand as a hermit. Carpentering on the main house, I had to work carefully, had to make sure the studs were plumb and the floor joists level. But I intended the Hovel to be out of square, free of geometry, indifferent to gravity. That's how I wanted to write, too, and that's the kind of place I wanted to write in, I told myself, every evening with my pens and notebooks, my cigarettes and six packs. The Hovel represented both a stoical little solitude and heedless self-indulgence. It was like a medicine cabinet in which I was doctor, patient, and disease. I could take off my masks in the Hovel, I imagined, and be raw me.

I was a small-time addict, really. I never got ugly, seldom staggered, only occasionally missed work. But tethered to the short leash of my habit, I was ugly enough. I would come home from work with a half case and a pack of cigarettes, and avoiding, if possible, any engagement with Kapa, I would head for the Hovel to write. I really did want to write, and I did fill pages, eked out a meager harvest of poems. But while the quality and quantity of my writing rose and fell, and winter followed summer in its tender round, my consumption of alcohol crept upward with a terrible linearity.

My father was not a particularly handy guy. I don't recall him doing many home repairs or carpentry projects. He liked to grow a few tomato plants in whiskey barrels, and he draped the cherry tree in the backyard with lengths and lengths of garden hose, believing the robins and starlings would mistake the hoses for snakes.

The only time I remember him using a hammer was one Fourth of July when I was four, or maybe five. This memory is unusually vivid: Dad had bought two huge shopping bags full of fireworks and invited friends for a barbecue. He pulled out a pinwheel, a firework you were supposed to nail to a post or a tree, where it would spin, shoot sparks, and whistle. My father didn't set down his cocktail to nail the pinwheel to the elm tree, but held glass and firework in one hand while he hammered with the other. When he lit it, the pinwheel sparked and whirled once and then leaped from the tree directly into one of the paper bags full of fireworks. Instantly, Roman candles and Blister Rockets and Chinese Pagodas blasted in every direction, kids and adults shouting and diving behind bushes. My father, drink still in hand, turned on the garden hose and doused his hundred-dollar show.

So it's plain that my interests in carpentry and gardening were not inherited from my father. Two things that I clearly did get from him were my love of reading and writing, and my alcoholism.

In 1933, long before I was born, Farrar & Rinehart published my father's first and only novel, *Cotton Cavalier*. The book won a prestigious national prize and was serialized in *Campus Humor* magazine. The protagonist of *Cotton Cavalier* is a college student named Peter. When the school's progressive biology teacher is fired for teaching evolutionary theory, Peter and his friends come to the teacher's defense. But when one of Peter's girlfriends accuses a Negro man of raping her, Peter and his friends lynch the innocent man. Though *Cotton Cava-*

lier seems dated now, caught up in the manners and rituals of small-town college students, the book's themes were courageous for the Depression-era South.

Some of the best writing in the novel is about drinking. After Peter helps in the lynching, he goes on a long, sustained binge. My father wrote, "By the trial and error method, Peter arrived at what to him was the golden mean of intoxication. He stayed just drunk enough to be agreeably muddled in his thinking. He never quite reached the state that is noticeable to others. Liquor as a sedative, however, had its disadvantages. He had to increase the doses little by little, had to be satisfied with a numbing effect instead of the former glow."

The photo on the dust jacket shows my father in a dark suit and tie, white handkerchief in his coat pocket, a long-stemmed briar poised in his hand. His high forehead makes him appear brainy, and his lips are full and sensuous. I suspect that he himself wrote the biographical sketch that accompanies the photo: "John Thomas Goodrich was born in Fayetteville, Tennessee, just twenty-six years ago. He matriculated at Bryson College, when it was still practicing the simple tyranny of the Old Testament. . . . Mr. Goodrich, as an expatriate Southerner, still thinks that fried chicken for breakfast is the nuts, and he'll take corn likker in preference to gin any old day."

A backsaw is a short, square-bladed finish saw, usually fitted into a miter box. The two-by-four I want Elliot to saw through is a heavier piece of lumber than a backsaw was designed to cut, but I know the backsaw's shorter length will be easier for him to steer, and the saw's fine teeth, while slow, will be less likely to grab at the grain and bind the saw. By the time he has cut the board clear through, the blond hair on his forehead is sticky with sweat, his forearms plastered with sawdust. He shakes his tired right hand as if trying to flick off a bug.

"It's not very straight," he says, wearily, and accurately, "but I did it. Can I stop now?"

"No, not yet. I told you, if you want a loft in here, you have to help me build it."

"Oh, all right."

I have him measure off another length, pencil an arrow-point at exactly 34⅝ inches, hold his plastic try square tight to the long side, and scribe the perpendicular line. When he's sawed halfway through he starts to tire, so I relieve him and finish the cut. The wood is incredibly hard.

"Wow, I didn't realize how dense this old, used lumber was," I tell him. "This is really difficult, isn't it?"

Elliot looks at me squint-eyed, tuck-chinned. "You mean, it's hard for you, too?"

"You bet it is. It's hard wood, hard work."

Before nailing the loft together, we predrill the holes. I steady the electric drill in place and Elliot reaches over my hands to pull the trigger. Next, with a few raps of his ten-ounce hammer, Elliot starts a sinker in each hole, and then I drive the big nails home.

The summer I was eighteen, between high school and college, I lived with my father in Fresno, California. It had been eight years since I had last seen him, in a hospital bed, sprouting the tubes and wires that were pumping him—slowly, tentatively— back from the brink of death. We'd traded letters over the years, so we knew enough about each other for small talk, but I was wary of him. He was white-haired and gaunt, his eyes bulged a little, and he wheezed with emphysema. But he was still very handsome, his courtly Tennessee manners more florid than ever.

The evening after my arrival I went with my father to one of his regular AA meetings, and sat sheepishly beside him as he introduced us.

"Hello, everyone, I'm Tom. I am an alcoholic. And this is my son."

It was his sixth AA anniversary, and he gave a short, prepared speech, a confession, really. He talked about growing up in Tennessee, going to college, moving to Chicago, biographical details I was already familiar with.

When he came to talking about his career as a writer, the publication of his novel, he said, "Success was the worst thing that could have happened to me, then. I became a big frog in a very little pond, and I couldn't drink enough to put things into perspective."

On the drive home, I asked him if he'd written any novels after *Cotton Cavalier*. The car slowed down a little. My father stared out over the steering wheel, gazing far off.

"No," he finally answered. "Only some fragments of bad ideas. I should never have written at all."

His voice was quavery, with self-pity, I thought, and it seemed as if he were speaking, not to me, but to some vast other, and I didn't like that.

Every morning in the last year before I quit drinking, I would start thinking about whether to get drunk that evening, and I'd come to the conclusion that that particular day would be a good one to not drink. But come five o'clock, I would drink, every day. I filled my Hovel notebooks with plans to quit, self-recriminations, less and less poetry.

Kapa and I fought relentlessly about whose turn it was to vacuum, to water the plants, to do the dishes, arguments all twisted to avoid the real issue, until finally, both of us confused and exhausted, Kapa moved out. We didn't see each other for a year.

I was lucky, in a way, to have my father's catastrophic example to sober me. His disaster prepared my deliverance. Elliot has not had to suffer the confusion and self-doubt of growing up in a household with a boozer for a father—my last drink was four years before he was born. But he may have inherited a susceptibility to alcoholism, he may have to suffer through the disease itself. Knowing that I've given him a haunted house to play in, that every father becomes a ghost in his son's closet, what more can I do than to teach him how to use some basic tools?

There's a photograph of my father and me I've always loved, but for many years I've kept it in a shoe box, because it pictures us together in a way that, soon thereafter, vanished forever: I'm five or six, sitting on his lap in the big overstuffed chair by the fireplace in our living room. There's a storybook open on my lap. One of my father's long arms is snugged around me, while with his other hand he's pointing up and away, toward the far corner of the ceiling, embellishing on the story. I'm riding his voice, peering after his gesture, my lips open a little in wonder, and my eyes wide—it's a look I've seen on Elliot's face—eager to believe whatever he tells me.

Nettles and Pines

Stinging nettles when you steam them are very tasty, like a meaty, slightly acerbic spinach. A pot of nettles signals for me the end of winter, when the season of gloom gives way to the season of cantankerousness, so I've come equipped with a pair of scissors and three plastic bags—one to put nettles in and two to serve as gloves. It's a warm and fragrant April morning, the river running high and muddy with recent rain. The nests of the great blue herons, fifteen or more—great rafts of twigs high in the cottonwood trees across the river—are almost hidden now by new foliage. I pussyfoot through a patch of yellow violets and white trilliums, don my glove-bags, and start snipping off the tender top leaves of nettles.

The first time I walked through this woodland, twenty years ago now, I thought it must be a remnant of the great riparian forest of ash swales, cottonwood stands, and willow thickets that used to border the entire length of the Willamette River. That forest used to stretch back from the river up to six miles on either side and it served to shade the river, trap eroded soil, and slow floodwaters. It provided habitat for all kinds of mammals, birds, reptiles, and invertebrates. But beginning with the arrival of Europeans into the valley in the mid-1800s, most of this forest was cut down and the fertile soils converted to agriculture, with little awareness of the long-term consequences. This strip of woodland had been spared, I imagined, because its many ravines and pothole ponds, its ragged, river-carved topography would have taken too much grading and filling to make it farmable. But I soon learned that in reality this whole bend of riverbank had been quarried for gravel. The ponds and ravines hadn't been scoured out by the river, but dug by bulldozers and backhoes and left unfilled when the gravel company went bankrupt. What I had originally thought was land carved by water was actually scarred by business.

The cottonwood trees don't care though. They grow fine on the mining spoils. The turkey vultures that roost in the cottonwoods don't care. They return to this place every spring, arriving just in time for lambing season on the valley farms, just in time for the flush of young possums and raccoons that will die in the woods or be killed on the roads. The nettles do fine here. Reed canary grass, an aggressive species that crowds out other plants, is happy here. The robins are whooping it up. And the rabbits and muskrats and little brown wrens don't

care if this land was abused. But I care. It makes me angry seeing how people have carved up this land for profit and left it in
waste. It's an anger I will try to use well.

I must have brushed against a nettle leaf as I was picking
earlier: I have a prickling welt the size of a quarter on my
wrist. Good. Let it fuel my resentment. I hear bulldozers
growling across the river at another gravel quarry, wreaking
their workaday havoc, robbing the river of the stones it's been
polishing for eons. I growl back at them.

Here I take a side trail out of the woods and come up into
the sports park, an enormous expanse of mowed grass, sten-
ciled with rectangles of white chalk, and with white mesh soccer goals placed strategically: the brand new Crystal Lake
Sports Complex. The field is huge, a quarter-mile wide by nearly
three-quarters of a mile long. It feels like a place apart, surrounded by tall trees and a hedge of wild blackberry bramble,
but it is less than a mile from City Hall, and the exhaust
plumes of the nearby fiberglass factory rise above the cottonwoods to the north. Behind me, beyond the belt of woodland,
flows the Willamette, while before me, to the west, a fifty-foot-
high bluff topped by a row of broken-crowned Douglas fir
marks the edge of the active floodplain. Crystal Lake, a eutro-
phying old oxbow going to willows, lies at the base of the
bluff, hidden in the woods. Atop the bluff lies Crystal Lake
Cemetery, and beyond it, my neighborhood.

Here in the floodplain, the soils are a luscious, deep, sandy
loam, fertile and well drained, and this field was still highly
productive after being farmed hard for well over a century.
But the town had grown around the field, and the farmer who
leased it had to drive his big machinery through downtown to

get here. The family that owned the land was interested in selling, and the city had an acute need for soccer fields.

I remember the day I met the farmer, Leo Martin, in the spring of 1996. I was a member of the city's Crystal Lake Task Force charged with designing the future park, and I'd been visiting the field as often as I could throughout the winter, monitoring the rise and fall of the floodwaters that, at their peak, covered three quarters of the acreage. One chilly March afternoon after the water had drained off, I walked down to the field and saw a big John Deere tractor idling near the gate. As I approached, a hulk of a man stood up between the culti-packer and the seed drill hitched behind the tractor. Leo Martin would be an imposing presence anywhere, a huge, blocky man, with a Hubbard squash of a head, bald on top but girdled with a shaggy furze of dark hair above his meaty ears. That day he was also drenched in hydraulic fluid, his clothes dark and clinging, his arms gloved in shiny, reddish-gray oil. If Elliot had been along, he would have added this giant to his catch-all category of power people, more awesome than a policeman, troll, Spider-man, or Luke Skywalker, for here was a flesh-and-blood, larger-than-life FARMER. I paused twenty feet away.

"Drilling wheat?" I called. I'd noticed the freshly furrowed bare soil where last month's floodwaters had drowned the fall-seeded wheat crop.

Leo waved a big crescent wrench at me, wiped at the oil smearing his forehead with the back of his hand, and came out to meet me. "Yeah. Tucking in some spring seed. It heads out the same time as the winter wheat, and yields almost as much." He pointed the big wrench toward his drill. "Third time that hydraulic hose has blown. Don't think I can mend it again."

Well, that was a lot of talking for a grass seed farmer, and it felt like a sort of a welcome, so I introduced myself. Leo wiped his enormous hands on a sopping shop rag but, thoughtfully, didn't offer to shake. When I told him I was a member of the task force that was planning the future uses for the field, he snorted.

"I don't understand why the city would want to put kids on this field. There's so much dieldrin in the soil, I had to quit growing pumpkins. And there's spots I could show you that just won't produce much of anything."

That seemed like an astonishing admission to make to a stranger. I wondered if he was pulling my leg. Or was he just being shrewd? Was he exaggerating the toxicity of the soil, hoping that people would consider it unsafe for soccer fields, thereby saving the land for farming? I knew that dieldrin was an insecticide related to DDT, banned in the United States in the 1980s. "What did you use dieldrin for?"

"Not me! When they grew hops here. In the '50s."

"And it's still in the soil?"

Leo twiddled the screw on his adjustable wrench and shrugged.

"So is this field important to you? If we put in soccer fields, will that be a setback to your operation?"

Another snort. "This field is a damn headache. Worse all the time. If it isn't the neighbors complaining, it's goose damage. I'm scared to grow corn here anymore. Remember what happened three years ago? Somebody brought a pickup in here at night and stole a mess of my corn and sold it to the Co-op Grocery as organically grown! Ha! I'd just sprayed the whole field for ear worm! Some people got sick, they told me. I don't know. I guess they caught the guy, but I didn't press charges. Wouldn't of done any good."

"What complaints do you get from the neighbors?"

"Neighbors! Ha! For one thing, the only way to spray this field clean is with a crop duster, an airplane. But, oh my golly, every time I had the duster out . . . did my phone ring!"

"Yeah, I was one of the callers. Five in the morning! It sounded like a war."

"Yeah, well. We don't do that anymore."

"How do you spray now?"

"We fly it on with a helicopter. At night."

That had to be a gully washer, but he never winked. Leo's stories seemed to be concocted of knowledge and opinions ground together like oats and alfalfa in a hog pellet, tough to swallow but highly nourishing.

"The city can have this field, and good riddance. Anyway, if they put it all to grass that should keep the geese on this side of the river, out of my home fields. Geese are killing me."

"But how much harm can a goose do?"

Leo looked at the sky, and whistled softly. Rivulets of sweat were eroding down through the oil on his forehead. I'd touched a nerve with the mention of geese, making him pull back and take stock. After a pause, he started back in more seriously.

"Let me tell you, mister: four years ago geese pulled up three quarters of my beet seedlings here. I lost thirty thousand dollars. Just them *walking* on a rye grass field will lower your yield 30 percent. They weigh eight pounds apiece, for god's sake, and they've got *big feet*! Used to be hunting would keep geese under control, but now things have gotten out of hand."

He rolled his massive head, crooked it to one side, reached over and gave his head a quick shove toward his shoulder. Vertebrae in his neck popped loudly, and he smiled. "We've found a new way to scare them off, though."

"What is it?"

"Can't tell you."

He could only have meant it was illegal, so I knew better than to ask further. Greedy as I was to hear more, it seemed time to call it a day. The light was going, the temperature dropping. I was shivering in my blanket-lined jacket. Leo, in a lightweight sweatshirt with the sleeves cut off midbiceps, looked to be steaming, sweat and hydraulic fluid making him glow like an overstoked furnace.

I stuck out my hand. "Hope we can talk again some time."

"Not likely," he answered. "I'm retiring. This is my last crop."

That was six years ago. Once the city bought the field, our task force held a mess of public meetings to solicit input on what to do with it. Some people wanted to pave an access road the entire length of the field with parking lots at both ends, and fill all 125 acres with sports fields. At the other extreme, some felt the whole field should be replanted with native trees. It took almost two years to hash out a compromise: the city would develop 40 acres for soccer fields and baseball diamonds, and 85 acres would be restored to native forest.

Just four years ago, I brought Elliot and two of his friends down here for a ceremonial tree planting to dedicate the forest restoration. It was a cold, showery March morning. The boys, in bright yellow and blue rain suits, slid through puddles, splashing muddy water all over each other. They'd already eaten a fair number of the sugar cookies provided for the occasion, and I was sure they'd need to be carted home soon and warmed up. So I quickly dug in my ten cottonwood seedlings and retreated to the shelter of the cookie canopy. I pulled another cup of coffee from the big urn and watched the two dozen or so volunteers still planting trees in the blustery rain.

For my city to purchase prime farmland and return it to native forest marked, it seemed to me, a sea change in policy and perception. The opposite trend—converting the Willamette Valley's riparian forest into farmland—had been until very recently supported by every notion of civilized conduct, as well as by persuasive economic incentives. It resulted in economic gain for farmers, but even more important, it was regarded as a virtuous utilization of the land, of benefit to the whole of the valley's human population.

The operative word, of course, was *human*. As I watched the boys squeal with glee in the mud puddles, and a group of neighbors, city employees, and utter strangers replant a future forest, I wondered if I was seeing a reevaluation of some of those old values, those civic and economic imperatives that had so radically reconfigured the land. Were we really beginning to understand all the unforeseen consequences of our industry? Were we already in the midst of rewriting our equations for what would be beneficial, in the long term, for humans? Might we even be widening our sense of what it means *to be human*? Or was I deluding myself to believe that more and more people seemed to recognize other species of plant and animal, and even the landscape itself, as fully alive, as aching with desires analogous to ours, and possessed of great intelligence?

Maybe after two cups of bad-urn coffee, I was just a cold and muddy man indulging in some wishful thinking. I shooed the kids away from the cookie platter and they went to play ring-around-the-rosy in a big puddle.

I recall an earlier ceremony, on a bright Saturday morning in June, when we broke ground for the sports field. There were three times as many people in attendance. A photographer from the local newspaper snapped pictures of kids in soccer uniforms turning ceremonial shovelfuls of earth. The Parks Department director thanked the mayor, the mayor thanked the city councilor and the city councilor thanked the parks director. The president of the fiberglass factory, looking exotic in his pin-striped suit and shiny black shoes, received the thanks of the mayor for leasing some land to the city for the parking lot. It was all quite festive. I felt a sense of gratitude to those people, allies and adversaries alike, aware as I was that the forest restoration project would never have been considered on its own merits, but had to be subsidized by the development of the sports fields.

Bulldozers, road graders, and belly scrapers were already working at the far end of the field. The Oregon National Guard's Engineering Corps had been enlisted to grade and contour for the sports fields. The sergeant major overseeing the project told us how pleased his boys were to perform this labor on behalf of our community. Then, just as the mayor began her concluding remarks, a belly scraper came lumbering straight toward us, closer and closer, until the mayor had to practically shout over the roar of the belly scraper's engine. The sergeant major scowled and fidgeted, and finally stepped out of our circle and vigorously waved the belly scraper away. It turned and lumbered back down the field.

The cottonwoods we planted that day four years ago have outgrown Elliot. The slower-growing ash, maple, and oak are thriving, too. One of the tree species that seems particularly happy here is the Willamette Valley ponderosa pine. I run my hand over the five-inch needles of a tree whose new candles when they lengthen this month are going to make the tree taller than me. For years I was unaware that ponderosas were ever native to the valley. I always associated them with the pumicey, well-drained soils of the high plateau of central Oregon. It turns out that a distinct subspecies of the ponderosa was abundant in the valley when Europeans began arriving, but the big, old straight grain trees were all quickly felled for lumber, and even the memory of them almost forgotten. Only in the past decade were a few old valley ponderosas tracked down and their seeds propagated.

Now we are bringing them back, replanting some of the great riparian forest. There will be big trees here for future heron rookeries. Our great-grandchildren will play soccer here, and the geese will look down at them as they power overhead.

But first, there will be nettles for supper.

Maintenance

As I paint the soffits high up on the east side of the house, three wasps fly around my head. They are long creatures, their abdomens connected to thoraxes by incredibly slender waists as if blown from black glass. Black-and-yellow mud daubers, I think. When I pressure-washed the siding last week, I knocked down several mud nests that were glued up under the eaves. These refugees fly listlessly around me, seeming to be more disoriented than aggressive, like stunned survivors of some catastrophe. Though I am not terribly afraid of being stung, I'm tense with the fear of falling. I can picture how it might happen, how I'd feel a sudden zinging pain in the cheek, drop the paintbrush and slap at my face, the ladder lurching sideways, the ground spinning up to meet me . . . So I keep half an eye on the wasps.

I am reaching farther than I probably should, trying to cover as much area as possible before I have to climb down and laboriously reposition my twenty-four-foot aluminum extension ladder. And now I've dribbled some red soffit paint onto yesterday's freshly painted gray siding. Wiping it off with a rag, I consider all the reasons why I hate painting. One, I hate the splatter-in-the-face of pressure-washing. Two, I hate the barked knuckles of scraping. Three, the gunked fingers of caulking. Four, the tedium of facing blank walls. Five, the tension of clinging to high ladders. Six . . .

A little bell rings behind me. I look over my shoulder and see Lucinda waving to me as she pedals her bike out of her driveway and down the street. Lucinda and her partner Raymond are the new owners of the house across the street from ours, Mrs. Trindle's old house. Propping my brush in the paint bucket, I turn around on the ladder and take a little break, consoling myself with the prospect of how far past painting their house is. The roof on Lucinda and Raymond's house is sheathed in blue tarps, a gutter dangles loose from the eaves, the broken screen door is tied open with baler twine. I can even see through the cracked picture window into the living room where the ceiling has collapsed, the Sheetrock gone to mush from rain leaking in. It was never much of a house to begin with and now it is almost past redemption.

It was built during the Second World War, knocked together in a few days along with hundreds more like it, as housing for the Adair Military Cantonment, a hastily assembled army base that sprawled over hundreds of acres a few miles north of town. The base was dismantled in the mid-1950s and many of the houses sold cheaply to whoever would relocate them. I don't know who moved their house, but Mrs. Trindle and her husband were already living here when I moved to the neighborhood in 1984. Mr. Trindle had mental disabilities that prevented him from working, and they were about as poor as you can get and still have a house and a car. Mrs. Trindle spent most every day visiting shut-ins, helping elderly folks who might otherwise have been forced to move into nursing homes. Then a couple of years ago Mr. Trindle died, but Mrs. Trindle kept on going, kept driving all over town to help other people, people who were probably not as poor or as alone as she.

By the time she finally decided to sell the place and move in with her daughter, the house was pretty far gone. Now Raymond and Lucinda are living in a travel trailer parked in the backyard while they consider whether to raze the house and start over, or try to pull it back from the brink. I don't think they have a lot of money, but they do have prodigious energy. Last week they started building a new pump house made of cob, a mixture of red clay, sand, and straw. Cob is like adobe except you don't form it into bricks; you just mix it and plop it wet onto the wall and let it dry in place. Elliot and I went over to help. Raymond would dump a wheelbarrow load of clay and a bucket of sand on a blue tarp, then add a scattering of straw and a splash of water from the hose. Our job was to mash it together with our bare feet. Elliot's friend Suzanne wandered over, shucked her shoes, and jumped in, and the two of them did the Mexican hat dance in the mud. After the cob was sufficiently smooshed, we'd scoop up a double handful and plop it onto the rising wall. Lucinda said they could go up a maximum of about two feet per day, which allowed time for each course to dry before the weight of the next layer was added on. Raymond told us there are cob houses in England that are five centuries old. I nodded with appreciation, but inside I shuddered at the thought of how many times in all those years such a house would have been repainted.

There's a writer I admire, J. B. Jackson, long-time editor of *Landscape* magazine, who has done a lot of straight thinking about houses. Jackson has suggested that the best metaphor for the average house is *an extension of the hand*. The house, Jackson believed, should be understood as "the hand we raise to indicate our presence . . . the hand that protects and holds what is its own. The house or hand creates its own small world; it . . . reaches out to establish and confirm relationships."

Jackson often expressed dismay over the near-total separation between our places of employment, our home life, and our wider social spheres, and so he especially liked to see small businesses operated out of some part of the house. Garage industries should be encouraged, he said, because they integrated work with domestic life, let the children, parents, and grandparents help and learn from one another. Business was best when conducted in the vicinity of "children and dogs and a vegetable garden, and the smell of supper being prepared."

For about ten years, a slow-talking old man named Fred ran a lawn mower repair shop out of Mrs. Trindle's garage. An archipelago of lawn mowers and old engines arced away from the corner of the house. There were always a few fixed-up mowers, rototillers, and an occasional washing machine standing in a row beside the street, offering themselves for sale.

Fred always wore a pair of overalls with an embroidered name tag that said "Ralph" in bright red stitching over the heart. That was Fred: no ego, just a pure penchant for fixing things. He was good, he was cheap, and we all mowed our lawns with Fredmobiles.

The tiny garage had just one light bulb dangling over the workbench. The shelves along all the walls bent down under dozens and dozens of coffee cans full of out-of-date hardware. In that unspeakable jumble of parts and debris, Fred could lay his hand on anything. I asked Fred once if he might have a used muffler for my old lawn mower. "Let me think a minute," he said. He set his pliers and screwdriver on the workbench, but kept his hands curled lightly around them as if they were some kind of divining rods. He closed his eyes and began searching through the shop in his mind. It might have been a minute, or it might have been two, but finally Fred walked past me to an old galvanized garbage can by the door, lifted out a couple of carburetors and some pieces of engine shroud, and retrieved a muffler, rusty but intact.

"Mine looks totally different than this one," I said.

"It'll fit," he answered.

My friend Rick lives on the other side of town in a very lovely house that has the bad habit of shedding. His house's wooden siding will not hold paint, regardless of the many professional remedies he's tried. So Rick's solution is to paint one side of the house every summer, spending each morning for two or three months pressure-washing, scraping, puttying, priming, and brushing on latex acrylic paint from the second-story eaves down to the foundation. Two summers ago when Rick was working on the later chapters of his most recent novel, and the writing was going painfully slow, I told him, "Rick, why don't you take a summer off? Give yourself more time at your desk. Your house won't begrudge you one year off."

"Nope," he said. "Out of the question."

Now, Rick is a very upbeat person, but he does grumble quite a bit about having to paint and paint and paint his house. So here I was, the messenger of liberation, giving him permission to skip one lousy year, and I was mystified why he would not even consider letting his maintenance slide. Over the course of the next few weeks my sane advice turned, I'm afraid, to pestering, and one evening Rick put his hand up.

"Look," he said, "maybe you'll think it's stupid, but I kind of *like* painting the house. Oh, not the pressure-washing, hauling the ladders around, certainly not the scraping. But once all the prep work is done, the painting itself isn't that bad." He looked at me moon-eyed, hoping I'd understand, but I gazed back blank as a wall.

"Well, really, it's like this," he went on. "When I'm painting the house, some of the older folks in the neighborhood have gotten into the habit of coming over while I'm working, and they talk to me, something they don't do much otherwise. And what they like to talk about is home maintenance, about painting and putting up new gutters and raking leaves and hosing down the driveway. And they all say that it seems like few of the younger people do that much anymore, and they sure appreciate seeing me out here working on my place."

It's a week later and I'm painting the window trim, definitely closing in on the finish, and I'm having to really keep a grip on myself to avoid getting sloppy. I'm not a good detail painter, as I am not a good finish carpenter. Kapa can't fathom how I can fuss over a line of an essay, trying to hide every trace of artifice, but be oblivious if the miter joints on my window trim are off by several degrees, leaving conspicuous gaps at each corner. But I am only an *amateur* carpenter, I tell her, as I am an amateur lover. My technique is lousy, but I've got *enthusiasm,* and I'm good at improvising.

I'm sympathetic to how Kapa must feel, though. After all, why would anyone *not* do the best job possible, especially on finish work? Honestly, I am sometimes ashamed of my impatience and my shoddy work, but I seem incapable of improving myself. It's true that part of the art of carpentry is to hide your work, to strive to make the seams and joints and nail holes invisible. But finish work is just not my forte. I'm a wood butcher, a quick-and-dirty carpenter, good at framing, at building trellises and gates, but lacking the patience and the fine hand-eye coordination to make perfect miter joints. I've had no real training as a carpenter, and not all that much experience. I own only cheap tools, and a kinky back. But none of those are my deepest reason.

The deepest reason that our house is full of gaps and cracks and knotholes is because, at heart, I like the faces of things to look their age, to wear their blemishes with dignity. I detect a wry smile in trim work that is slightly askew. Moreover, I could never have begun building this house if I hadn't allowed myself to start with the humblest standards and then let them drift steadily lower and lower. Perfectly mitered joints would have sealed up my sanity. Those gaps in the trim are escape valves, where my spirit whistles free.

I do have my scruples. If I bend a nail, I don't keep bludgeoning it, trying to bury it in the wood. My carpenter friend Elmer taught me some tricks for dealing with bent nails. First off, once a nail bends, subsequent blows are not likely to set it back on course. Even if you tap the nail sideways to straighten it, or take the claw and try to twist the nail back to its original shape, or, your best technique, use your slip-joint pliers to carefully unbend the nail exactly where it is bent, your next tap, however carefully aimed, will likely bend the nail again. That's because when you first bent the shaft of the nail, you also bent the *head,* and subsequent blows won't be transmitted directly. So you need to flatten the head out, put it back perpendicular to the shaft with little, well-aimed jeweler taps of your hammer. After you've straightened the shaft and flattened the head again, hold the shaft at the weak point with your pliers. Now you should be able to drive the nail home. But if it bends again, pull it and start over.

I once had a dentist with big, misaligned buck teeth that made for the sweetest, easiest, most unprofessional grin. He was a good tooth doctor, but it was his smile that won me over. Then, after twenty years in the business, he had his front teeth pulled and replaced with a perfect bridge. I haven't been back to him since. Give me the crooked tooth, the mole on the cheek, the scar on the lip. Give me the crow's feet that jump out like living sparks from around Kapa's eyes. Give me the calluses on her knees. Do not expect me to master finish carpentry.

Though I've always loved houses with that down-at-the-heel look—moss-covered shingles, cockeyed screen doors, a front porch leaning comfortably toward the grass—I don't know how to square my taste for things much-loved-but-run-down with my desire to keep Knot House ship-shape-and-good-as-new. Not long ago I visited a friend whose house was visibly sinking into the earth, an old farmhouse, steep roofed with tall windows in the upstairs gable ends. Its clapboards had sprung loose here and there, the chimney was crumbling, the roof swayback and rotting. I could picture how it must have been in its prime, painted a cheerful butter yellow, the green shingles bright as new leaves. But now the roof, the walls, even the windows were a splotchy gray-brown, the same color as the bark of the craggy maples overhanging the eaves.

Although the occasion for my visit was a garden tour, I asked our host if I could see the inside of her house, and separated myself from the others. I felt a powerful attraction to this house and I wanted a few moments to understand, or at least identify, the welter of emotions it was stirring in me. Behind the front door, a scythe was hanging by its blade from a too-small nail. Muddy footprints lead to the kitchen. Here all the counters were buried under jars of home-canned cherries and plums, pickled green beans and mushrooms. Fruit flies cruised above plastic buckets full of vegetable rinds and egg shells destined for the compost. Bundles of herbs hung from the sagging ceiling. Stacks of cookbooks and seed catalogs cluttered the plank table. Strong and conflicting smells of onions and lavender, honey and wet wool, rusty iron and mildew made me feel slightly drunk. A faucet dripped and a clock ticked. I stood there trying to sense what this house was telling me, when suddenly my stomach knotted in pain as I realized how rapidly this house was dying. The jumble of feelings inside were of the same dark hue as those I'd felt when I sat with

Andrew in the last weeks of his life, watching his joyful spirit sink into foreboding and his probing mind grow knotted with confusion as the tumor grew ever larger in his brain.

I fled outside, back to the garden, joined the others as they sampled fruits in the raspberry patch. I listened as our host told how she made her compost, that wonderful story of the resurrection. I found a clutch of ladybug eggs on the underside of a comfrey leaf, and showed them to Elliot. And gradually that moment of lacerating awareness I'd felt back in the moldering kitchen grew over with a tougher skin. I realized, there in somebody else's garden beside a wonderful but tumbledown house, that the time was not that far off when Kapa and I would find it difficult to keep up our house. Already the gardens were almost beyond our upkeep, the grass and weeds creeping in at the edges, the wild blackberries taking root inside the hedges.

How likely was it, I wondered, that Elliot would want to live in Knot House when he grew up and had a family of his own? Not very. I tried to imagine putting the house up for sale. But we sure as hell wouldn't let a realtor on the premises. We'd find a suitable buyer ourselves, somebody who'd treasure the gardens, who'd find the knotty floor and the poorly mitered window trim comfortable, endearing. *Look,* I'd tell them, *here are all the original blueprints. Look, here is where I smashed my thumb with the hammer—there's blood smeared on the two-by-four behind this sheetrock. Look, Kapa tried five different colors on the bedroom walls before she discovered this perfect shade of peach. And right here, right here in the living room, this is where Elliot was born.*

Would prospective buyers listen to the stories that come with the house, or would they think that the house was just a big wooden box with windows? It would be hard selling Knot House.

I'm done. The last of the trim is painted, brushes are all washed, ladders put away in the woodshed. It's a clear, early September morning. I sit in the herb garden in the fragrant shade of the clerodendron, nursing a cup of coffee, watching the chickadees peck ripe seeds from the sunflowers in the garden. Knot House looks very spiffy in its fresh paint, a youthful bloom restored to its cheeks, though I notice that the asphalt shingles are beginning to curl. We'll need a new roof in a few years. I did the roofing the first time, going on twenty years ago now, but I hope to spare my knees the next time. Roofing is a job for younger hands.

There's a wonderful moment at the end of Michael Pollan's book, *A Place of My Own,* when the little writing house he has been building for two years comes alive. He is rubbing furniture oil into his new, built-in desk. "Bringing nothing more than my hands to the task, I slowly rubbed and pressed the wood as if it were muscled flesh, over and over again in a widening spiral of attention. And after a few hours it did begin to feel like some weird interspecies form of massage. The backs of these boards, far from being inanimate, responded to my touch, absorbing the oils and then admitting the light deep into their grain . . . There are boards in this building already as familiar to me as the skin on the back of my hand." The house has come alive. The end of building is the beginning of living, the beginning of never-ending maintenance and remodeling. In fact, maintenance began the moment construction began, and remodeling began the moment you pulled out your first bent nail.

I've always believed in the vivifying power of touch, believed that the house needs the hand to animate it. But J. B. Jackson says the house *is* a hand. He sees the house as reaching out to its community. I try to think of the houses on my street as holding hands. Some of them are very uncomfortable, and a few of them simply refuse. But our houses and ourselves are all connected by the street, by the power lines and phone lines, by the air we breathe and the water we drink, by the robins and the squirrels who trespass so happily across our property lines, by our children, by our mutual interest in safety, freedom, the desire to thrive, by the touch of the stories we tell one another.

It's a kind of maintenance, to tell stories. It keeps the greater household of the community in tune. Maintenance invokes a cyclical worldview, the house again and again restored to youth. Maintenance: the word means literally "to hold in the hands." I hope my paint job lasts many years. And I trust that the wasps are rebuilding their nests under the eaves.

Epilogue: *The Cardboard Castle*

As I weed the garden, I watch Elliot wreck his castle. Wearing the new forest-green tunic that Kapa made for him, brandishing the sword he and I knocked together from scrap lumber, he stabs and whacks at the cardboard. I spent four solid hours building that castle, and though I gave him permission to knock it down today, watching him destroy it brings up some unexpected feelings: I have a knot in my jaw and my gut is rumbling. I hack at the spring weeds with my hoe.

The castle was my gift to him for his eighth birthday party. I started calling local appliance dealers in early April, asking them to save the cardboard cartons from refrigerators and washing machines, and by the first of May I had stockpiled a dozen. Then on the morning of Elliot's party, I started building. The four tallest boxes I placed upright at the corners. Next, I made each wall of the castle with two boxes laid end to end on their sides. That made an open square nearly twelve feet on a side with a grassy courtyard in the center. Next, using a carton knife with a fresh blade, I sliced the main entry into the front wall, twin doors arched at the top. Then I crawled inside and started cutting passageways one by one between all the adjoining boxes, strapping them together as I went with lots and lots of packing tape. As the morning progressed, it got stifling hot in there, and a sharp, sour smell came off the cardboard. It took a couple of hours, cutting and taping, crawling from one box into the next again and again, until my back muscles got twangy and my knees ached.

Once the basic structure was stitched together, I added a second tier of smaller boxes to the corner towers and topped them with pointy roofs made from four triangles of cardboard taped together. I crawled through one more time and sliced out two more doorways—a back door and an entry into the court-yard—and some little windows here and there. I had planned to cut out some crenellations for the roof, but I ran out of time. Kapa added a couple of pennants to fly from the ramparts. The interior of the castle was a long rectangular tunnel the kids could crawl through. They could stand up in the corner towers and poke their noses out little windows I'd cut high up. When the whole party of ten girls and boys arrived and jostled in-side, the castle shook like a chrysalis ready to split open.

Every day since the party, a week now, Elliot has played in his castle. One day Johnny came over and they played pi-rates—the castle a ship—and repeatedly kidnapped me at sword point as I worked in the garden. Another day Suzanne and Elliot drew eyes, stars, moons, and flowers with Magic Markers on the cardboard walls. Each day Elliot asked if he could wreck his castle, but I kept saying, no, let's get a little more life out of it. Then two days ago it rained, and the castle began to sag and twist, began to look more and more like something out of a fairy tale, a run-down old heap wherein some enchanted princess slept.

"Papa, watch this," Elliot yells. Getting more ambitious about razing his castle now, he backs up, runs forward, and leaps onto the lowest box. A whole section crumples under his weight. He runs and leaps again and again. Having ridden down several walls, he rolls over on the vanquished cardboard and, looking to see if I've been watching, punches his fist triumphantly in the air. I raise a fist back to him, without gusto, and hoe more furrows for bean seed.

I watched two guys take down a nice old house in the center of town a few years back, dismantling it stick by stick to sell the used lumber and fixtures. I bought some siding for my shop from them. It was already a hundred years old when I bought it, and it's still holding up nicely. When the two men were done, there was nothing but a rectangular foundation left on the ground, just the ghost of a house surrounded by lilacs and forsythia. And more than once I've seen a decent house flattened by a bulldozer and the refuse hauled away to the landfill. The death of the dismantled house seemed meaningful, but the deaths of those bulldozed houses seemed like murder.

Only one last corner tower of the castle is still standing. Elliot has disappeared inside it. I sneak over and listen at the walls.

He is still spinning out his story, softly and rapidly, almost singing. Although I can't make out his words, I can tell by the lilt and rhythm that he's making up a spontaneous fantasy with himself as hero. His models are King Arthur, Robin Hood, Indiana Jones, Luke Skywalker, and his stick is a magic weapon—sword, rifle, or light saber. He wields it now for good and now for evil, trying on different roles, sensing the different valences of power and peace. Through these fantasies he is calibrating his moral compass.

I wonder if he will ever think of making a home as heroic adventure, as a brave and daring endeavor. Lord knows we need heroes on the home front. There are houses to build, gardens to cultivate. There are communities to grow, habitats to restore, splintered families to help heal. And then there is the inner frontier—the wilds of the heart. Will he discover the joys and terrors of exploring his own soul? The practice of home opens that way, as well, no end to obstacles and opportunities.

Now he comes flying out of his tower, sprints a dozen yards away, stops and turns slowly, hand resting on the hilt of his sheathed sword. I see his lips working, the story still unspooling from deep within him. He stands very still and calm, a moment of equipoise. All of a sudden he races back toward the tower and leaps at the wall of his former hideout. In moments, the last of the castle lies flat on the ground.

I'm glad it's over with. I rake up my pile of weeds and wheelbarrow them to the compost.

Lately I've been thinking about adding on again, building a larger bedroom for Elliot. Better yet, maybe he and I could build it together. His present bedroom is very small and it won't be long before he is bumping his head on his hanging loft bed. I have the design for the new room all worked out. It is the same room I sketched eight years ago while Kapa was in labor, the day Elliot was born. Trying to understand my place in that burgeoning new world of babies and family commitments, I turned to a fresh page in my journal and sketched the dimensions of a room, a new study for myself, a room I could fill with books, a room I could disappear into and do my own creative labor.

But it makes more sense for the new room to be Elliot's. He needs more space. And besides, if we build him a new room, then maybe I could reclaim his bedroom for my study. I still prefer writing in a smaller space where my thoughts can't drift too far before they bounce off a book and come back a little better educated. The upstairs study where I work now is a lovely room, but the many windows are often distractions to me. I have gradually piled books higher and higher on the shelves surrounding my desk, walls of books, so that by now I can barely see over them to look out the windows. I sometimes scold myself for not reshelving my books more frequently, but I see now that I've actually been building a vessel to write in, a more intimate interior space, a cell made of books to help me concentrate and to dream, to spiral inward and outward in search of the meaning of home.

Elliot isn't quite old enough to do much of the actual carpentry yet. But if we wait another three or four years, building the room together might make a great passage into adolescence for him. He could have a larger bedroom that he had a hand in designing and building himself. He could help us draw the blueprints, apply for a permit, work up the lists of materials, get bids from the lumberyards. Maybe we could invite other people to come swing a hammer, too, people who are important to him in his life—his friends, his older cousins, some of the neighbors, a few of Kapa's and my adult friends who have been close to Elliot. We could have a room-raising party.

I can't wait too long, though, because I am reaching the far cusp of my carpentering years. The constant ache in my knees, the crankiness that enters my wrists and shoulders when I split wood tell me this. It may be I'll have to serve as general contractor, walk around with the blueprints rolled under my arm saying things like, "Measure twice, cut once, son," and scolding anyone who isn't wearing eye protection. I could run to the lumberyard for more nails, and bring back coffee or soda pop for the whole crew. As everybody leans back on the freshly framed stud wall and mops the sweat from their brows, I'd hoist myself onto a saw horse, and start in on a story— "Yep, when I first came here, this was just a vacant lot . . ."

Suggestions for Further Reading

Alexander, Christopher, et al. *A Pattern Language* (New York: Oxford University Press, 1977). If you are one who loves particular architectural places, reading Alexander will illuminate *how* those places make you love them, and you'll want to create such places in your community.

Bachelard, Gaston. *The Poetics of Space* (Boston: Beacon Press, 1969). No one can look at a house and see the poetry of human longing like Bachelard.

Cline, Ann. *A Hut of One's Own* (Cambridge: MIT Press, 1997). Cline was trained as an architect, but she was most original as a ceremonialist. Cline's quirky book is to Alexander's *A Pattern Language* as a haiku is to Walt Whitman.

Colebrook, Binda. *Winter Gardening in the Maritime Northwest* (Seattle: Sasquatch Books, 1989). Among those who are less susceptible to winter depression in the rainy Pacific Northwest are mushroom hunters, steelheaders, and the mud-splattered students of Colebrook's gardening book.

Jackson, J. B. *Landscapes: Selected Writings of J. B. Jackson,* edited by Ervin H. Zube (Amherst: University of Massachusetts Press, 1970).

Kahn, Lloyd. *Shelter* (Bolinas, California: Shelter Publications, 1973). A scrumptious compendium of pictures and information about handmade houses the world around.

Lopez, Barry Holstun. *Giving Birth to Thunder, Sleeping with His Daughter: Coyote Builds North America* (New York: Avon, 1981). Do not build your own house without consulting Crow, Beaver, Coyote, and the other resident helpers and tricksters in your mythic neighborhood.

Pollan, Michael. *A Place of My Own* (New York: Delta, 1998). "To build a house in the first person, a place as much one's own as a second skin, would require an exploration of self and place," says Pollan, an explorer of the first order.

Proctor, Jody. *Toil* (White River Junction, Vermont: Chelsea Green Publishing, 1998). Proctor wrote dozens of never-published novels, then put together this hilarious and dead-on memoir about his year building houses with a small, family-run construction company.

Rudofsky, Bernard. *Architecture Without Architects: A Short Introduction to Non-Pedigreed Architecture* (New York: Doubleday, 1964). A photo essay on vernacular architecture—yurts, caves, homes hollowed out of trees—featuring grainy, black and white snapshots of marvelous eloquence.

Snyder, Gary. *The Practice of the Wild* (San Francisco: North Point Press, 1990).

_____. *A Place in Space* (Washington, D.C.: Counterpoint, 1995). No one, to my mind, has done more than Gary Snyder to illuminate the potential for approaching ordinary life as a spiritual practice.

Starck, Clemens. *Journeyman's Wages* (Ashland, Oregon: Story Line Press, 1996). These wry, plain-spoken poems by a long-time journeyman carpenter insist that manual labor can be a sacramental act.

Thoreau, Henry David. *Walden and Other Writings.* My battered Ballantine paperback edition has copious underlining and marginal notes from my long and contentious apprenticeship to Thoreau, but lists no publication date. I know I bought it in 1973. This edition has a fine introduction by Joseph Wood Krutch.